I0110686

Traditional Witches' Book of Love Spells

Angela Kaelin

2012
Winter Tempest Books

Copyright © 2012 Angela Kaelin

All rights reserved.

ISBN-10: 0615729142
ISBN-13: 978-0615729145
Winter Tempest Books

DEDICATION

In memory of my grandparents.

CONTENTS

CHAPTER 1
ABOUT LOVE SPELLS

Casting love spells is a wonderful way to bring more beauty and romance into your life. Love is vital to health and happiness and the desire for romantic love is a natural human trait. The spells in this book are intended to help you fulfill your innermost desires for love and passion.

There is no special time or circumstance that is right for love or romance. Whenever you feel you are ready for a relationship with another person, you are ready. Use these spells to find a yet unknown love or to transform a friendship into a romance.

Love is a very important and highly personal matter. If you are looking for love or are already in love with someone, you may have other people telling you that romance is not that important. Sometimes friends will try to discourage you from relationships with other people because of their own selfishness or feelings of jealousy or envy. Family members may even try to interfere with your happiness. Use these love spells to stop interference from family, friends or enemies who would interfere with your personal happiness.

People who are in love should not be kept apart, nor

should people be forced to remain together when there is no love. So, let no one dissuade you from finding the love you desire or from moving on when the time is right for you to do so. Use these spells to find the love of your dreams and bind him or her to you or to discourage an unwanted relationship.

No moral judgments are made in this book. It is presumed that every person is acting in accordance with his or her own will and that any desires they have to be in a mutually agreeable relationship with another consenting person are in accordance with the nature of the universe itself.

Love spells fall into different categories and may accomplish their purpose in slightly different ways.

Types of Love Spells

Glamour Spells: Make yourself more attractive and desirable with these spells, which work on both subconscious and subtle energetic levels.

Spells to Find an Unknown Love: Open your own subconscious, activate energies and send them into the cosmic ether to surround your future lover. When these subtle energetic emanations find resonance, the purpose of the spell will be fulfilled. These spells don't work overnight, but they do work.

Spells to Attract a Particular Person: Send out energy to a specific person. Many of these spells work by means of telepathic hypnotic suggestion. If the suggestion is strong enough and persistent enough and not completely against the will of the subject, it can be very effective.

Spells to Bind a Lover to You: Intensify an existing romantic relationship. Includes aphrodisiacs and love philters. These spells affect both the spell caster and his or her lover.

Spells to Reunite Lovers: Bring back a lost or wayward love.

Commanding Spells: Tame and control a lover who may be jealous, have a wandering eye or who is engaging in other unwanted behaviors.

Break-up Spells: Cause discord between a couple or cause a break up or divorce. These spells tend to be a little darker in nature and are intended to affect only the two people you want to break up. There are, also, spells here to get over a past love affair.

Spells to Banish Unwanted Persons: Discourage unwanted attention from a past lover or other person. These spells can be used to discourage and protect yourself against disturbing or undesirable behaviors on the part of an former lover, a stalker, harasser, persistent colleague or other pest. They work by protecting you and sending discouragement to your oppressor. The intensity of this spell should be consistent with the level of the offense. And, practical action should be taken in consideration since such people can become dangerous. There are, also, spells here to end a worn out and undesirable love affair.

Safety with Incense Burners and Candles

Some spells call for loose incense to be burned. You do not need a charcoal disc to burn loose incense, even if the spell calls for charcoal. The oldest and purest form of incense involves lighting loose herbs and resins. But, many people like to use charcoal discs. If you have never used one of these before, the following information is especially important:

Take special care with charcoal discs; they are not like stick or cone incense. Charcoal becomes exceedingly hot; it can melt linoleum and can cause damage or even a fire. If you use charcoal, place it in a charcoal-safe burner or small iron cauldron with legs. Place the burner on a brick, a ceramic tile or a marble cutting board. You can, also, place it in a box of sand, which will safely absorb the heat. Always use charcoal in a ventilated area because it produces toxic fumes.

Take the usual precautions with other incense and burners. Take care when burning them around pets or children. Never leave them unattended. Never go to sleep with a candle burning. And, heed all the warnings on the packaging.

Burn candles and incense in safe places, on surfaces that are sturdy and where the items are not apt to be knocked over or fall. A fireplace is often a safe place. Alternatively, a box of sand is a good, safe way to arrange and burn both your candles and incense.

Safety with Herbs and Essential Oils

Please, bear in mind that just because an ingredient is natural or not widely recognized as toxic, this doesn't mean it is safe for all people. Any herb can cause an adverse reaction in some people.

For instance, there are people who are allergic to the entire mint family. Although, plants from the mint family are not generally thought of as being toxic.

Some herbs and especially their essential oils are not safe for human consumption. A few of the ingredients in these formulas are caustic and should be handled with care. The magical love potions in this book are not intended for consumption with the exception of the legendary love philter Love Potion No. 9 and some tea recipes.

Where a known toxic ingredient is mentioned in the list of love herbs, the author has tried to place a warning about it. But, there is no way to guarantee a potentially dangerous ingredient has an adequate warning. If you are in doubt about an herb or ingredient, check its safety before using it.

Many essential oils and some herbs, including those with names ending in "bane," are toxic, even deadly, if consumed. Essential oils should never be applied to children approximately three years of age or younger or to cats. Pregnant and nursing women should, also, take special precautions and completely avoid some herbs and oils as they can affect the delicate hormone balance.

Angela Kaelin

CHAPTER 2
HOW TO CAST SUCCESSFUL LOVE SPELLS

To succeed at casting love spells, you must first decide exactly what you want to accomplish. Then, look for relevant spells and choose the one best suited to your particular personality and needs.

While the subconscious mind or the power of suggestion may play a role in the efficacy of spells, they mainly work according to the theories of esoteric science called "magic." The official scientific paradigm has no explanation for it. Nonetheless, magic is the result of natural forces that involve the concept of a dynamic ether, which is a universal energetic fluid, through which directed energy can pass in much the same way as a satellite signal or radio wave is transmitted.

For a love spell to work, it requires a great deal of concentrated mental and emotional energy, which is directed squarely at the target and then released, just as a bowman releases an arrow.

Any spell has these three aforementioned elements: (1) Concentrated energy; (2) directed mental focus or *will*; and (3) release.

A spell helps you to generate the appropriate energy for

your purpose by gathering items that have a corresponding energetic frequency. Colors, gemstones, herbs, symbols and other items all have an energetic frequency, which is directed by the action you take in the spell. Some spells help you to accumulate energy by working to build up power over a period of days before a final release is made.

The actions you take in the operation of casting a spell help you to direct your mental focus or *will* at the subject. Some spells require a picture or possession of the person in order to create a focal point for your energy.

Whether explicitly instructed or not, every spell requires you to release the energy. This is why sometimes items are buried, hidden, tossed away or you simply turn your back and walk away. The idea is that it is done and forgotten.

Most of the time you will not see instantaneous results from your spells. This is because it takes time for the subtle energies to manifest in the dense energy of the physical world we live in.

Spells should be done in secret. The thoughts of others, even inadvertent ones, are projections of energy that may be disharmonious with the purpose of your spell. Always try to choose places where you can work undisturbed and give your full attention to your work.

Once you understand how spells work, you can alter them a little bit to suit yourself. The most important part of any spell is not the objects you use or the actions you take, but how well you can focus your concentrated energy, direct it at your target and release it.

With any of these spells, you may want to begin by conducting your own ritual to clear space or use a bundle of white sage to smudge the area. The smoke from the white sage will neutralize any interfering energies. It can, also, be used to cleanse your candles, crystals and other items before you use them.

Many spells call for you to dress a candle with an oil preparation. When you do this, keep in mind the purpose of your spell. If you are trying to attract something good into your life, dress the candle by applying and stroking the candle toward you. Conversely, if you're trying to get something out of your life, stroke the candle in an outward direction, away from you.

Oils used in genuine magical preparations are essential oils, which are real extracts of plants, each of which have their own particular energy. Fragrance oils are artificial chemicals that do not possess the appropriate energy. Do not use fragrance oils in spell work.

Beneficial Timing

Most spells to attract love are conducted on Friday or Sunday, during the waxing or full moon. When in doubt about timing, you may generally rely on these days and moon phases as good choices. But, there are specific days, which may be more beneficial depending on the exact nature of your intention.

In general, if you are trying to draw something toward you, you should do a spell when the moon is full. If you're trying to get rid of something, do your spell when the moon is waning.

Friday is the day of Venus and a propitious day for most love attraction spells. Saturday is the day of Saturn and is associated with decrease and reduction. Sunday is, of course, the day of the Sun and is associated with family and true happiness.

Some practitioners choose odd numbered hours of the day to conduct spells because they consider them to be more powerful than even numbered ones. Multiples of three are regarded by some as especially powerful.

The minutes after sunrise on any day are the most powerful time to perform spells associated with the influences of that day.

Days of the Week

Use this guideline to determine a beneficial day upon which to conduct your spells

Sunday (Sun): Family and marriage contracts

Monday (Moon): Matters surrounding the home and family

Tuesday (Mars): To increase passion; courage and domination

Wednesday (Mercury): Matters involving communication

Thursday (Jupiter): To encourage and expand on an existing romance

Friday (Venus): For spells involving matters of the heart; romance; beauty and friendship

Saturday (Saturn): To bind; banish; curse or hex a lover; to break up a couple; to get revenge and reverse spells

Moon Phases

Moon phases and days of the week are given here as a guideline. Spells may still work if you don't pay attention to them, but they may work better if you do.

New Moon: This phase runs from the first day of the new moon to 3 1/2 days after. It is a good time to conduct spells to attract love, passion, lust and romance.

Waxing Moon: This phase begins 7 days after the new moon and lasts for 7 days. It is the right time to conduct spells to attract love or enhance a current romantic relationship.

Full Moon: This phase begins 14 days after the new moon and lasts 3 1/2 days. It is a good time to conduct spells to find love or romance and for fertility, protection and divination.

Waning Moon: This phase begins 3 1/2 days after the full moon and lasts for 10 1/2 days. It is the right time to conduct spells to hex, bind, get revenge, break a habit and to banish a pest, an enemy or an unwanted lover.

Dark of the Moon: This phase begins 10 1/2 days after the full moon and lasts for 3 1/2 days. It is a good time to conduct spells for getting rid of a lover or to heal a broken heart.

The Moon in Astrological Houses

Another way to determine the best time to conduct love spells is based on the characteristics of the moon in the twelve signs of the zodiac. Almanacs give the signs of the moon throughout the calendar year and some web sites offer "Moon Sign Calculators" you can use to determine the position of the moon for any day of the year.

Beneficial aspects of the moon for love spells are as follows:

Moon in Aries: Spells to increase passion and to dominate a situation or person

Moon in Taurus: Spells for practical; every day matters.

Moon in Gemini: Potions related to communication and healing

Moon in Cancer: Spells involving the home; fertility; family and children

Moon in Leo: Glamour spells; avoid conducting love attraction spells at this time

Moon in Virgo: Spells for security and stability

Moon in Libra: Spells pertaining to marriages; partnerships and peace keeping

Moon in Scorpio: Spells regarding divination; the dark arts and sex-related matters

Moon in Sagittarius: Spells involving travel and learning; avoid doing spells for divination or psychic enhancement at this time

Moon in Capricorn: Spells for domination; control and stability

Moon in Aquarius: Spells for healing; peace; harmony; understanding

Moon in Pisces: Spells involving divination; spirit communication and emotions

Timing plays a role in other aspects of life on this planet, such as planting and harvest times. So, it is no wonder that spell casting is affected in a similar way. The old alchemists noted that certain experiments failed at certain times and succeeded at others, although sometimes they were not sure why. In the same way, you should approach spell casting as an experiment.

Preparation for Performing Successful Love Spells

Places accumulate psychic energy, which may either be a help or a hindrance to your ability to attract and sustain love in your life, depending upon its nature. Negative thoughts, whether your own or those of others, even those who may have lived or worked in a place a long time ago, may accumulate and work against your attempts to bring love and happiness into your life. It is important to clean these out before you begin to create a more positive energetic environment.

If you are experiencing bad luck in love or if you feel that your home life is not as happy and harmonious as you would like, consider doing a house cleansing and protection.

In order to attract more positive energy, your home and work place should be organized and free of clutter. Physical dirt carries its own vibration, which may interfere with the harmonious environment you want to create. Therefore, regularly dust, vacuum and sweep. If you have wooden or tile floors, you may add a few drops of essential oils like Rosemary and Lavender to your cleaning products to clean on an spiritual level as well as a physical one.

As you clean, imagine the negative energies dissipating. If you sweep with a broom, open the door and sweep the dirt out, visualizing all of the negativity going out with it. When you clean the dirt from your vacuum, visualize it as negative energy as you dump it outside your home.

Traditionally, house washes like the following formula, which is brewed as a tea or decoction and strained, may be used as mop water for inside and outside the house. If it is strained through very fine filters, it may be placed into a spray bottle and sprayed around the house for protection. Take care not to saturate fabrics or carpeting and ventilate the area well until the moisture dries.

House Cleansing and Protection

1 gallon pure Water
1/2 cup Peppermint
1/4 cup Angelica root
1/4 cup Basil
1/4 cup Sage
1/4 cup Hyssop

Combine the above ingredients and bring them to a boil. Reduce the heat and allow this potion to simmer for several minutes. After it is cooled, strain it and use it to wash down the inside and outside of your home.

Mop inside and out. Use a clean cloth to wipe down all of the surfaces, to cleanse them of their old adversarial vibrations and bring new ones, which are harmonious with your purpose.

Ways to Create a Peaceful Environment

Living houseplants and flowers in the house help to create a more positive environment.

Regularly burning high quality incense or using a diffuser that disperses essential oils raises the spiritual vibration of a place. Diffusers filled with essential oils of Peppermint, Basil, Eucalyptus, Lavender and Rosemary serve a dual purpose of destroying bacteria and mold in the air at the same time.

Crystals may be charged and blessed for protection and placed around your home and outside. Blessed sea salt or Holy Water may be sprinkled inside and outside the home.

It is not absolutely necessary to do any of these things, but it is something to consider, especially if your home has been the scene of arguing, violence or other unpleasantness that could leave a lingering energetic impression. It is more difficult to achieve positive results when a dark cloud seems to be hanging over a place.

A common, effective way to clear a place of negative energy is to light a bundle of White Sage and allow the smoke to drift around every room in your home. Afterward, follow a similar procedure with a braid of Sweetgrass to invite helpful spirits back.

Creating an Altar or Work Space

Many spells in this book ask you to do work at an altar or work space. You do not have to have a fully equipped altar to cast spells successfully. But, it can be helpful to have some of the proper tools and equipment and a place to conduct your work. It is important to have a clean work space where you can do your spell and leave it undisturbed for as long as necessary.

People who live alone are at somewhat of an advantage when it comes to spell casting. Not only do they have more time to practice gathering and focusing energy and more room to do their spells without the interference of others, but they have the luxury having work space that will remain undisturbed by others over the course of days that it may take to conduct a spell.

Couples and families often like to have a special room in their homes dedicated to ritual and spell work. Those with less room to spare set up an altar in an inconspicuous part of the house. The benefit of this is that the area, once spiritually cleansed, remains relatively clean because people are not walking through it.

The altar usually features blessed and consecrated items such as:

An athame or double-edged knife
A cauldron
A censer or thurible (incense burner)
A chalice
A crucible
Wands for different purposes such as ceremonial or for the direction of specific types of energy
Candles and candle holders
Images and other symbolic representation of helpful spirits

Typically, the elements are represented in some way. The following are examples:

Earth: Salt and sometimes a pentacle, which is, also, used to represent the fifth element
Air: The wand and incense
Fire: The athame and flame of the candle
Water: A cauldron or goblet filled with water

These representative objects are sometimes employed to charge other objects. For example, objects are charged by sprinkling them with salt, passing them through incense, directing energy at them with the athame or sprinkling them with water.

The expectation is, also, set up by the spell caster that once in the designated room or at the altar, only certain things such as meditation, rituals, invocations and spell casting are going to take place. This is a good way to both psychologically and energetically reinforce your purpose.

While the aforementioned ritual items are all valuable, many if not most of them are entirely optional and used at the discretion of the practitioner.

Casting a Circle

Casting a circle is optional for most spells, however, it is something people like to do, especially when they feel there are forces working against them or they simply need additional reinforcements.

Many Wiccans cast circles to draw upon the power of their gods and center themselves in an energy vortex, which is sometimes called a cone of power. The Hermetic Order of the Golden Dawn ritual is similar to that used by Wiccans, but slightly more complex. Other ceremonial magicians cast simple circles for both power and protection, from within which they safely and effectively communicate with spirits.

Similarly, the Obeah practitioners of Africa and the aboriginal magicians of Australia, also, cast protective circles to facilitate spirit communication. Casting a circle may, also, be helpful to you if you are having difficulty focusing or meditating.

There are many ways to cast a circle ranging from the very simple to the complex, but the Wiccan method is very popular.

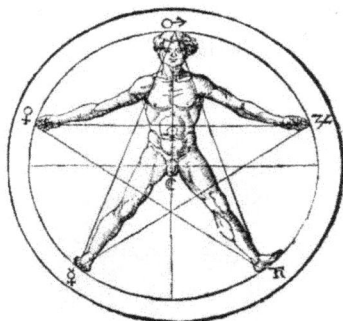

A Wiccan Circle

This circle-casting ritual varies slightly from practitioner to practitioner and coven to coven. The following is a simplified version, which you can use to call the elements, to generate power and for protection from adversarial energy. Use it at your discretion to enhance your spell work.

You will need four candles. Ideally, they should be of four different colors: Red; black; white and blue, however, four white candles will do.

Most Wiccans open and close the circle facing north, but older variations on the ritual open and close facing east.

Draw a circle on the floor, mark it out with masking tape or draw it using the point of an athame or wand and simply visualize it. Use a compass to find the four directions, then place a candle at each point. If you are using colored candles, place the black candle at the north, the red candle at the east, the white candle at the south and the blue candle at the west.

North and black represent the earth
East and red represent fire
South and white represent air
West and blue represent water

Stand facing north in a powerful stance with your feet a comfortable distance apart, raise your arms in the air, palms facing outward. If you have an athame, hold it in your right hand and say, "All hail the Guardians of the Watchtower of the North. I call upon you, the powers of earth, to guard and oversee this operation." Afterward, trace a pentacle in the air with your right index finger or with the athame.

Then, walk to the east and repeat this procedure, except you will say, "All hail the Guardians of the Watchtower of the East. I call upon you, the powers of fire, to guard and oversee this operation."

Then, walk to the south and repeat this procedure, except you will say, "All hail the Guardians of the Watchtower of the South. I call upon you, the powers of air, to guard and oversee this operation."

Then, walk to the west and repeat this procedure, except you will say, "All hail the Guardians of the Watchtower of the West. I call upon you, the powers of water, to guard and oversee this operation."

Return again to the north and trace the pentacle one last time before walking into the center of the circle.

To trace the invoking pentagram, begin at the bottom left hand point, move to the top point, down to the bottom right hand point, to the left-hand point, to the right-hand point, and back to the bottom left hand point.

Do not go outside the circle, but perform your spell within it. You should have all the things you need already there within the circle and ready to be used.

After you have completed this operation, close the circle by starting in the north, again. Then, walk in the opposite direction, thanking each power for its presence and bidding it to go in peace. Address each element as follows, "Spirits of the north, I thank you and I bid you go in peace," as you go around the circle.

Trace your banishing pentagram as follows: Begin at the top point and move down to the bottom left point to the right point, to the left point, to the bottom right point and back to the top point.

A Simple Circle

Circle-casting rituals all incorporate the concept of the four elements, which are the spiritual precursors to life on the physical plane, to form a circle that represents the universe itself with you as the creative force within it. But, your circle does not have to be created through an elaborate ceremony to be effective.

If you feel you need the extra protection and power of a circle, simply draw a circle on the floor using chalk, tape, your ritual knife or simply your finger. Some old-fashioned conjurers made two concentric circles of a similar size and wrote the names of angels or the Tetragrammaton around the circle's edge.

For the circle to be effective, you must see it as a representative of the universe itself, with yourself in the center of it as its master. Gather power into the circle through the charging meditation of fire and water, as discussed in the next chapter. Use this circle to become completely focused on your purpose or as a powerful place from which to plan or conduct your spells or communicate with spirits.

The circle can, also, be used for a love drawing meditation. Light a red candle, dress it with Cinnamon oil or an appropriate Love Drawing Oil and meditate on the fulfillment of your needs and desires.

Uncrossing

Sometimes love spells fail because the person is crossed, which is another way of saying hexed or jinxed. In most cases, this is not caused by malicious witchcraft, but negative energy that has accumulated around the person, which needs to be cleared before lasting success may be achieved.

Crossed people may experience setbacks and difficulties, not only in romance, but in other areas of life. Uncrossing spells may be used in cases where nothing seems to work or positive results seem to be only temporary. They are used in cases where you feel there are energies attached to you that are working against you or when you have the feeling that you might be jinxed.

For most people, the matter of uncrossing is a simple one that involves nothing more than taking a spiritually cleansing bath like the Uncrossing Bath below.

Afterward, if you still feel in any way disturbed or have a sense of not being aligned with your true purpose and desires or if you feel that you have received a lot of negative messages from your family or others about relationships and your ability to find and sustain love has suffered because of it, then you may want to perform the entire Uncrossing Spell for a period of seven nights.

There are fairly rare cases, depending on your cultural background or associates, in which a person is actually hexed by a witch. Black magicians place such curses and only through knowledge of black magic and the dark arts can they be successfully resolved. But, they are unusual and more than likely you would know if you had become such a victim.

Fortunately, the vast majority of people are simply a little bit energetically contaminated at times. This is not due to any fault of the person or their wrong-thinking. Nor, is it the result of a curse or hex consciously placed by another person. More often people simply accumulate energy that is not conducive to the attainment of their goals and this must be cleansed before real progress can be made.

Uncrossing Spell

An Uncrossing Spell is a mild form of exorcism. There can be layers to the negative energies, so it may take any number of workings before they are completely purged, however, you are likely to feel a strong sense of relief immediately after performing this spell for the first time.

You will need the following:

White candle
Uncrossing Oil (formula below)
Uncrossing Bath (formula below)

Anoint the candle with Uncrossing Oil, using a motion away from you. As you work the oil into the wax, visualize all of the negative energy surrounding you and all of your unwanted subconscious programming about love and relationships going into the oil and permeating the candle.

Uncrossing Oil

1 cup Almond oil
7 drops Bay oil
7 drops Hyssop oil
7 drops Lavender oil
7 drops Rose oil
7 drops Verbena oil
7 drops Vetivert oil (or a root may be added to the master bottle)

Make this oil by adding the above drops of essential oil to the Almond oil. If you do not have the essential oils, but you have the dried herbs, you may make this formula by adding a handful of each of the herbs to a pint or so of oil and allowing it to remain in a warm place for a couple of weeks. Strain the liquid and place it in a dark bottle with a tight lid. Always store your potions in a cool, dark place.

After you have anointed the candle, take an Uncrossing Bath.

Uncrossing Bath

Make a traditional Uncrossing Bath by brewing a strong tea using a handful each of Bay leaves and Hyssop blossoms. You may, also, add Rose and Lavender blossoms for calming and increased protection. Sage and Lemon are other herbs commonly used in Uncrossing formulas. Add these herbs or essential oils to your Uncrossing Oil or bath formula at your discretion.

Allow the herbs to boil in a gallon of pure water for several minutes before removing the mixture from the heat. Allow it to cool and strain it before adding any essential oils.

Recite the following incantation over the brew before adding it to your bath water:

"Purge me with Hyssop, and I shall be clean; wash me, and I shall be whiter than snow."

Alternatively, you may, also add a few drops of Uncrossing Oil to plain liquid Castille soap like Dr. Bronner's to make an Uncrossing Bath.

You may use this simple Uncrossing Bath right before conducting any spell. Some practitioners, also, use a bath like this one after working malefic spells to rid themselves of any negative energy they may have acquired.

After you have completed your bath, light your anointed candle and recite Psalm 51 in its entirety, as follows:

"Have mercy upon me, O God, according to thy loving kindness; according unto the multitude of thy tender mercies blot out my transgressions. Wash me thoroughly from mine iniquity, and cleanse me from my sin. For I acknowledge my transgressions; and my sin is ever before me. Against thee, thee only, have I sinned, and done this evil in thy sight; that thou mightest be justified when thou speakest, and be clear when thou judgest. Behold, I was shapen in iniquity; and in sin did my mother conceive me. Behold, thou desirest truth in the inward parts; and in the hidden part thou shalt make me to know wisdom. Purge me with hyssop, and I shall be clean; wash me, and I shall be whiter than snow. Make me to hear joy and gladness; that the bones which thou hast broken may rejoice. Hide thy face from my sins, and blot out all mine iniquities. Create in me a clean heart, O God; and renew a right spirit within me. Cast me not away from thy presence; and take not thy holy spirit from me. Restore unto me the joy of thy salvation; and uphold me with thy free spirit. Then will I teach transgressors thy ways; and sinners shall be converted unto thee. Deliver me from blood guiltiness, O God, thou God of my salvation; and my tongue shall sing aloud of thy righteousness. O Lord, open thou my lips; and my mouth shall shew forth thy praise. For thou desirest not sacrifice; else would I give it; thou delightest not in burnt offering. The sacrifices of God are a broken spirit; a broken and a contrite heart, O God, thou wilt not despise. Do good in thy good pleasure unto Zion; build thou the walls of

Jerusalem. Then shalt thou be pleased with the sacrifices of righteousness, with burnt offering and whole burnt offering; then shall they offer bullocks upon thine altar."

If you are planning on conducting this ritual for more than one night, snuff out the candle after a couple of hours. Otherwise, simply allow the to candle burn out, secure in the knowledge that, as it does so, it destroys any negative energy that may have surrounded you.

Repeat this procedure in preparation for casting spells or whenever you feel out of sorts, stressed or anxious.

Angela Kaelin

CHAPTER 3
HOW TO CHARGE OBJECTS

A spell book is really little more than a recipe book. It can tell you which items to use, what words to say and when to conduct a procedure, but there is a one vital element that only the spell caster can supply to the operation. This is your own condensed and focused psychic energy.

No spell book can tell you everything you need to know to make a spell work because the real magic comes from within. This is a power derived from both knowledge and practice in the art and science of controlling the elements and applying mental force to them.

The two main elements you must concern yourself with for the purpose of charging objects with psychic energy are fire and water. When we speak of elements in this way, we are not referring to actual fire and water, but to esoteric concepts that possess similar qualities. Terms like earth, air, fire and water are not to be taken literally. Although they are sometimes used symbolically in spells or rituals, it is only to remind practitioners of these esoteric concepts and not to create a worship or reverence for the actual earth, air, fire or water of the physical world.

Within every atom and within you, two principle forces

are at work, one is electronic and fiery and the other is magnetic and watery in nature. These elements are called fire and water respectively and refer to the electromagnetic force within all of nature, including the metaphysical world. Here, again, nature does not refer to the great outdoors, but to the universal construct as a whole.

It is these two elements that create a powerful force within you which you can direct in order to gather energy and charge objects. It has unlimited other uses, as well, but within the scope of this book, we will only discuss its use in spell casting.

When you wish to say a prayer, make a petition, send energy to someone or impregnate an object with the force of your will, begin by gathering energy.

How to Gather Energy

The two elementary principles, fire and water, are similar to the properties in a battery. One has a positive charge and the other one has a negative charge. The fiery principle repels and exerts force in an outward motion. The watery principle, attracts and exerts a magnetizing force in an inward motion. This repelling and attracting, in and out motion is the nature of the electromagnetic force.

It is necessary for you to be able to quiet your mind and focus for just a few minutes at a time to charge an object.

Relax yourself by taking a couple of deep breaths and releasing the tension from your body.

Put your mental focus on the place inside your body on your spine behind your navel. With each breath pull the element of fire, the active component of electromagnetic energy out of the environment and form it into a little ball in the pit of your stomach. Keep growing this energetic ball with each breath, which you will see as a ball of bright white light, slightly tinged with a vibrant shade of red. Keep growing this ball and condensing its power.

Then, while holding this ball there in the pit of your stomach, begin to accumulate the water element from the environment around you and add it to the existing ball.

This energy is tinged with blue and green and it swirls around like smoke as you gather it out of the air and pull it into the dense ball of energy. Do this until you have a more or less equal amount of fire and water element gathered in this ball.

After you have done this for a minute or so, draw in a little bit of earthy dark red and gold energy to bring the vibratory level down just slightly. This helps to make the energy more dense and physical.

This is how you gather electromagnetic energy. Using your imagination, you can now cause the ball of energy to disperse and go down into the ground. Or, you may continue with the operation of charging.

How to Charge Any Object

Place before you the object you want to charge, whether it is a candle, a potion you've created, a glass of water or any other object you might use in a spell.

Close your eyes for a moment and imagine the entire world as nothing more than a sea of vibrating energy. Imagine that you are zooming your focus in on a tiny spinning atom and project your mind into the center of it. What you find there is an electromagnetic force, which is tinged by the nature of whatever thing it is a part of.

It is on this subatomic level that you will be projecting your energy into objects. These objects function as multidimensional holograms and like holograms, if you affect one part of it, you affect the entire thing.

You may open your eyes or keep them closed while charging an object. Hold the object to be charged or place your hands over and around it. It doesn't matter how you do it, but you must force the ball of energy you accumulated to move through your body, out of your hands and finger tips into the center of the atoms of the object. Alternatively, you can project it straight out of your abdomen by means of a visualization where it simply pours directly out of you and fills the form of the object before you.

Once this is done, the object is energized with the electromagnetic elements of fire and water. You must now project your mental powers upon the energy in the object and impregnate it with your will or desires.

Suppose, for example, that you want to charge a candle, which you plan to burn as part of a spell to find the perfect man or woman for you. You will be burning this candle, which will probably be red or pink to represent your desire for love. The smoke from the candle, which is its essence, will be carried into the outer environment to impregnate the energy around it with your desires.

Begin by filling yourself with energy as previously instructed. Then, direct the accumulated energy into the object. With your mind's eye, see the energy filling every atom of the candle. Focus your energy on the candle and nothing else. Once you have filled the object completely, impress your desires upon the vibrating force you have placed within it.

Speak the object as if it were a person. Say, "Now, you shall become an instrument for my will. You are to find and return to me the love that I desire." Or, you may only use the force of your thoughts.

Once you have done this, you may end with the word, "Amen," or the phrase, "So mote it be" or whatever words of power you might want to add to this procedure. Your object is now fully charged with your focused energy and impregnated with your intention by force of your mind or your will.

How to Make and Charge a Talisman

A talisman is an object you carry with you, usually under your clothes and touching your skin, which is empowered with specific energies intended to attract or repel a certain condition.

In the following chapters, you will find information about herbs and gemstones along with formulas you can use to make a type of talisman commonly called a mojo bag.

Other types of talismans are made of engraved metal and are widely available from metaphysical stores and jewelry-makers. They include talismans like one of the Venus talisman from old grimoires like the "Greater Key of Solomon" as well as little figurines, animal totems or saints.

Magic squares or kameas are talismans drawn on paper using incorporating numerology. Runes and other symbols are used to make a variety of talismans for different purposes that can be charged and carried, used in spells or placed into a mojo bag with your selected herbs and stones.

Design your own personalized love talisman by acquiring or making a little cotton or flannel mojo bag about 3" x 5" and filling it with stones and herbs, which possess the energies you want to bring into your life.

For example, if you want to create a talisman to draw true love, place the herbs from the True Love potion (Elecampane, Mistletoe and Verbena) into a red linen, flannel or cotton bag or into the center of a red handkerchief and tie it with a ribbon or cord.

If you want romance, add a small piece of rose quartz to your true love talisman.

If you want to dominate your lover, then you might want to add a whole, unbroken High John Root to your bag. Direct the power of the High John root for a specific purpose by anointing it with a particular oil such as Calamus for added domination power plus a Love or Domination Oil.

Regardless of what type of talisman you choose, it must be fed from time to time by being anointed or passed through incense, specific to your objective. When you anoint or feed your talismans, don't just go through the motions or rubbing on the oil or waving it through the cascade of incense smoke, but gather your energy and pour it into the object, then impregnate that energy with the force of your will or desire by telling it mentally or verbally what you want it to do.

Sympathetic Magic

Most spells make use of what is called sympathetic magic. This is the occult science of correspondences or similarities between objects. This is why we make use of plants whose leaves or blossoms have certain appearances or other properties similar to the influences we want to bring to a working.

Effigies, poppets or "voodoo" dolls are dressed with items that have a similarity to the influences we want to bring to bear on a situation. Photographs, blood, hair, nail clippings and personal items are objects that carry a similar vibrational harmonic to the person associated with them.

What is at work here is sometimes called the "Law of Similars," which is used in homeopathy. This means that like can be used to influence like. We find objects that have a vibrational frequency similar to the type of action we want to bring to bear and we manipulate and exert that force on objects that are vibrationally similar to that which we wish to influence.

For example, if you wanted to dominate your lover, you would obtain something that has his or her vibrational signature on it. This might be a photograph or a piece of paper with his or her signature on it. You would conduct your spell using a doll or a red candle to represent your lover and attach the item with his or her similar vibration to it. Or, you might work with the photograph or paper alone.

To make a lover behave in a certain way, you would act upon this vibratory representation in a way that represents what you want to happen in the physical world. You would influence his or her personal vibratory rate from a distance using powders, oils and other substances that impart energies conducive to your purpose.

You might do something to symbolize your domination, using your own blood or other bodily fluids together with a dominating potion.

Afterward, you would apply this potion to the image, candle or other object that carries your lover's similar vibration, charge the objects concerned with your energy and impregnate that energy with your will, as previously described.

In this way, you are effectively influencing your lover's mind and emotions. When you act upon the object that represents his or her energetic vibration, it as if you are acting upon the actual person.

Understanding the Theory Underlying
Successful Spell Casting

To get the most out of your efforts, it helps to understand the basic magical theory behind spell casting.

Every spell should be conducted with the most energy you can conjure and direct into the operation. The energy of your emotion should be focused upon your purpose by your thoughts. After you have put a great deal of energy into your spell, you must release it. Essentially, this is done by emitting either a burst or a sustained flow of energy, then afterward forgetting about the entire issue. This is why you are frequently instructed to bury an object or place it somewhere to be forgotten.

Specific herbs, minerals and other objects are employed in spells because of their innate energy. If you apply this similar energy to an object that has the similar energy to the object you are trying to affect, for example, yourself, your lover or your home, then you are affecting one energetic form by another through sympathetic magic. Distance healing, also, works on the same principles. So does distance harming.

This same principle is elegantly stated by Aleister Crowley in the famous quote, "Love is the law, love under will." Love means resonance, harmony or an energy with a quality similar to that you want to work with. Love under will is a reference to manipulating this energy with your mind.

So, the process of performing any magical working involves the following:

1. A clearly defined objective

2. Harmonic similarity or resonance with the action you want to produce through the use of candles, herbs, gemstones, etc.

3. The object to be acted upon or its representative, for example a photograph, a spot of blood, hair or personal article

4. Charged intention, directed by the mind or the will upon the objects employed in the spell

5. A final, complete release of this energy

This final step is important. Once a spell has been performed, if the energy involved is held onto by the spell caster, it will never have the opportunity to work. Your will must be released into the outer environment to influence the universal vibrational field. In many spells it is released through burning and allowing the essence of the charge to be carried through the air, liquid being poured out into the earth, buried or hidden away.

The more you perform spells and work with the ideas of sympathetic magic, energetic gathering, charging, willing and releasing, you will naturally develop your own ways of doing things within the bounds of the laws of occult science. Read more about sympathetic magic and charging objects in the book, *How to Write Your Own Spells for any Purpose and Make Them Work*, by Sophia diGregorio

CHAPTER 4
LIST OF LOVE HERBS AND MINERALS WITH THEIR PROPERTIES

Use this reference for additional ingredients for your potions, spells, mojo bags and other magical workings.

A- E

Acacia (twigs and bark): To awaken new love and enhance psychic powers and physical strength
Adam & Eve Root: Love; happiness and binding
African Violet: Release harmonious love vibrations
Agaric: Fertility
Aloes: Love and spirituality
Amber (Ambergris): Courage; longevity; success; lust; inspiration; psychic powers and wealth
Angelica: To banish a rival and to receive visions of a future love
Apple: Love; healing and immortality
Apricot: Love
Aspen: Keep a lover from being stolen
Aster: Love
Avens: Love and purification

Avocado: Love; lust and beauty
Bachelor's Buttons: Love; worn to attract romance
Balm of Gilead: To increase the strength of other herbs in a love spell
Banyan: Good luck; fertility and good health
Barley: Love and fertility
Basil: To keep lover from being stolen; fertility; ashes of burnt leaves are added to love potions
Bedstraw: Love
Beech: Love and tolerance
Beet: Love and good health
Bergamot: Aphrodisiac
Bing Cherries: Divination and love
Birth Root (Beth Root): Love; marriage; romance; domestic peace and harmony; ease of childbirth
Bishop's Weed: Protection from snakebite and to provoke lust
Bistort (Snakeweed): Fertility and to increase psychic powers
Bittersweet: Protection and to heal a broken heart
Black Snakeroot: Love; lust and wealth
Bleeding Heart: Potent in all forms of love magic; used for love divination
Bloodroot: Love; purification and protection
Blue Cohosh: To attract love
Buckeyes: Luck finding love
Brazil Nut: Love
Byrony: Binding
Calamus (Sweet Flag): To dominate a person or situation
Camellia: Love and luxurious wealth
Camphor: Divination; spiritual cleansing; healing and past lives
Caper: Lust; luck and to increase potency of spells and potions
Caraway: Lust; protection from thieves and increased psychic powers
Cardamom: Love and lust
Carnation: Love; strength and protection from evil

Carrot: Lust; fertility and health
Cat Tail: Lust
Catnip: Love; beauty; happiness; relaxation and to make an unfaithful lover faithful again
Cat's Claw (Una de Gato): Youthfulness; healing and protection
Celery: Lust; increased mental powers and psychic abilities
Cerato: Self-confidence
Chamomile: Purification; harmony and good luck
Chaste Tree Berries (Vitex): Love and fertility control
Cherry: To enhance psychic powers; clairvoyance; dreams; creativity; love and healing
Chestnuts: Love and a peaceful home
Chickweed: Love and fertility
Chicory: To receive favors and increased psychic abilities
Chili Pepper: Love; hex breaking; fidelity and to expedite the action of a spell
Cinnamon (bark): Power; confidence; lust; aphrodisiac and increases the action of potions
Clary Sage: Visions; divination and love
Clover: Fidelity
Cloves: Glamour and fast money; to banish a rival; divination; aphrodisiac; vigorous action
Cocoa Beans (Chocolate): Love; euphoria
Coltsfoot: Love and divination
Columbine: To reunite lovers
Copal: Love; to attract a very pure love; divination; purification and to attract spirits
Coriander (Cilantro): Romantic love
Corn: Protection; fertility; good luck and divination
Cotton: Love; good luck and psychic abilities
Couch Grass (Witch Grass): Binding; love and dark arts
Cowslip: Glamour; youthfulness and to increase desirability
Crocus: Visions; increased psychic powers; to promote peace and attract love
Cubeb: Love

Cuckoo Flower: Love and fertility
Cucumber: Healing; fertility and chastity
Cumin: To keep a lover faithful and ward off evil
Curry: Protection
Cyclamen: To forget a lost love; to reinforce a current romance; fertility; lust and protection
Cypress: Protection and longevity
Daffodil: Romantic love
Daisy: Love; to return a lost love and induce flirtatiousness
Damiana: To intensify passion; attract a new love and cause a lover to return
Damill: Love and lust
Dandelion: To fulfill secret longings; break hexes; call spirits; psychic dreams and divination
Date Palm: Fertility and potency
Deer's Tongue: Lust and seduction
Devil's Bit: Love; lust; protection and exorcism
Dill: Love; lust; wealth; protection and to break a love spell
Dittany of Crete: To inspire love in another person; manifestations and astral projection
Dock: Money; fertility and healing
Dodder: Love and divination
Dogwood: Love and lust
Dragon's Blood: Love; confidence and to restore sex drive in men
Dulse (Kelp): Protection; peace; harmony; lust and health
Dutchman's Breeches: Love
Elder Bark: Protection; prosperity; exorcism; to break hexes and to bring a wealthy love
Elder Flower: For beauty and protection of property
Elecampane: Love; protection and to increase psychic powers
Elm: Love
Endive: Love and lust
Eryngo (Eryngium): Love; lust and peace
Evening Primrose (Oenothera biennis): Love and comfort

F-P

False Unicorn: Protection of mother and child; lust
Fava Beans: To make wishes come true
Fennel Seeds: To attract love and protect from malefic witchcraft
Fenugreek seed: Beauty and breast enhancement
Fig: Love; fertility and divination
Fleabane: Protection; fidelity and exorcism
Fuzzy Weed: Love and successful hunting
Galangal (Low John): Love; courage; protection and to drive away bad luck
Gardenia: Love; peace; healing and spirituality
Garlic: Protection of the home; exorcism; lust and to prevent theft
Gentian: Love and strength
Geranium: Love; wealth; power; fertility; courage; protection and good health
Ginger: Love; power; protection; success and restful sleep
Ginger Grass: Aphrodisiac; healing; causes mood changes
Ginseng (Wonder of the World): Love; beauty; strength; health; protection and aphrodisiac
Golden Rod: Love and luck
Grains of Paradise: Love; lust; inspiration and good luck
Grapes: Money; fertility and wishes
Grass of Parnassas: Love and joy
Hawthorn: Fertility; fidelity and happiness
Heather: Love and binding
Hemlock: To destroy the sex drive (Poison: Do not ingest)
Henbane: To attract love (Poison. Do not ingest)
Hibiscus: Lust; love and divination
High John the Conqueror (Ipomoea Jalapa): For domination; commanding and to attract love
Holly: Love; binding; protection and powerful dreams
Honeysuckle: Love and prosperity
Houseleek (Live Forever): Love; protection and good luck
Hyacinth: Love; happiness; protection and peace
Iron Weed: To control others

Ivy: Binding; protection and healing
Jasmine: Love; to heal heartbreak; for inspiration and prophetic dreams
Job's Tears: Good luck and to make wishes come true
Joe-Pye Weed: Love and to inspire respect
Juniper Berries: Love; good luck and exorcism
Kava Kava: Love and protection
Knotweed: Binding
Kola Nut: Peace and happiness
Lady's Mantle: Love
Leek: Love; protection and exorcism
Lemon (leaves): To evoke longing and love; for purification and immortality
Lemon Balm (Melissa Officinalis): Longevity; love and success
Lemongrass (Cymbopogon): Lust and psychic powers
Lemon Verbena: Love; luck; purification; to increase the potency of potions
Lettuce: Love and divination
Licorice: Love; lust and fidelity
Lime: Love; happiness and protection
Linden: Love; luck; protection; sleep and immortality
Linseed: To keep a lover faithful
Liverwort (Trefoil): Love and protection
Loosestrife: Peace and protection
Lotus Pods: Protection and to break love spells
Lovage: Eroticism; to draw love and success
Love Seed: Love and friendship
Maguey: Lust
Magnolia: Fidelity and past lives
Maidenhair: Love and beauty
Male Fern: Love and luck
Mallow: Love and protection
Mandrake (European): Love and protection; used as an effigy (Poison. Do not ingest)
Maple: Love; lust and longevity
Marjoram: Love and health
Meadow Sweet: Love; happiness; peace and divination
Mimosa: Love; protection and prophetic dreams

Mint: Good luck and to attract helpful spirits; aphrodisiac
Mistletoe: Love; fertility; to break hexes; exorcism and a successful hunt (Poison. Do not ingest.)
Molasses: Binding
Moonwort: Love and wealth
Mullein: Love; courage; divination and exorcism
Myrtle: Love; fertility; youthfulness and peace
Neroli: Love; matrimonial bliss; good luck and to make one more attractive
Nettles: To break up a relationship; exorcism; protection and to inspire lust
Nuts: Love, fertility and prosperity
Oak: Good luck; fertility; potency; exorcism and protection
Olive: Lust, fertility; strength; protection and peace
Onion: Money; prophesy; lust; exorcism; aids in recovery of strength after severe trauma
Orange: Love; insight; meditation; divination and happiness
Orange Blossom: Romantic love; happiness; divination and binding
Oregano: To ward off interfering in-laws
Orchid: Love
Orris Root: Love; protection and divination
Pansy: Love and divination
Parsley: Love; protection; binding and purification
Parsnip: Sex magic for men
Passion Flower: Friendship; peace and to calm nerves
Patchouli: Lust and fertility
Paw-paw: Love; protection and revenge
Pea: Love and money
Peach: Love; fertility; longevity; exorcism and fulfillment of wishes
Pear: Love and lust
Pennyroyal: Strength; protection and peace (Caution: The essential oil is poisonous. Do not ingest.)
Peony: Protection and exorcism
Pepper: Protection and exorcism

Peppermint: Purification; exorcism; love and psychic powers

Pepper Tree: Protection and purification

Periwinkle: Love; lust; protection and fulfillment of wishes

Persimmon: Sex and lust

Pimento: Love

Pimpernel: Protection, especially of emotions and family relations

Pineapple: Luck and to keep a lover true

Pine Needles: Protection; cleansing; fertility and exorcism

Pistachio: To break love spells

Plantain: Protection and strength

Plumeria (Frangipani): Love; to attract the admiration of others and garner trust and openness

Pomegranate: Fertility; divination; good luck and wishes

Poppy: Love; fertility and persuasion

Prickly Ash: Love and to break hexes

Primrose: Love; to intensify romance; protection and to compel a person to tell the truth

Purslane: Love; purification and protection from psychic attack

Q-Z

Quassia: Love

Queen Anne's Lace: Love and to strengthen the bond between two people; used to control fertility

Quina Roja (Cascarilla Colorada): To inspire lust in another person

Quince: Love; protection and happiness

Radish: Protection and lust

Raspberry (leaves): Love; protection and good luck

Rhubarb: Protection and fidelity

Rice: Money and fertility

Rose: Love; lust; healing; luck; courage; protection; prophetic dreams and to increase psychic powers

Rose Alba: Love and insight

Rose Geranium: To stop gossip and false accusations; to reverse negativity

Rosemary: Lust; love; mental power; exorcism; purification, youth and to gain control of a man

Rue: Exorcism; increased mental powers and to break hexes and love spell

Rye: Love and fidelity

Safflower: Purification

Saffron: Love; lust; strength; psychic powers and happiness

Sage: Youth; immortality; wisdom; protection and wishes

Sagebrush: Purification and exorcism

St. John's Wort: Love; strength; happiness and protection from malefic witchcraft

Salep (Lucky Hand): Luck and protection

Sampson Snake (Black Sampson): Love; virility; to enhance masculinity; power and success

Sanicle (Saniculus Europaea): Love; to keep a lover; safe travel and healing

Sarsaparilla: Love and wealth

Senna: Love and to expedite the action of a potion

Sesame: Lust and happiness

Skullcap: Love; fidelity and peace

Southern Wood: Love; lust and protection

Spearmint: Love; healing and increased mental powers

Spider Wort: Love and binding

Spikenard (Nardostachys Jatmansi): Love; protection and strength

Squaw Vine: Fertility; childbirth and to protect children from the evil eye

Strawberry: Love; happiness; luck; aphrodisiac

Sulfur: Hex breaking; protection and to break someone's control over another person

Sugar Cane: Love; lust and to gain sympathy

Sumbul: Love; luck; health and to increase psychic powers

Sunflower: Wisdom; fertility; health and wishes

Sweet Grass: To call good spirits

Sweet Orange: Love and divination

Sweet Pea: Love; courage; fidelity and friendship

Sycamore: Revitalization
Tamarind: Aphrodisiac
Tansy: Love; longevity and protection
Tarragon: Confidence; courage; domination; love; passion; strength; protection and to prevent theft
Thyme: Love; longevity; courage; divination and to increase psychic abilities
Tomato: Love
Tuberose: Love and peace
Turnip: Protection and to end a relationship
Trumpet Weed: To increase male potency
Unicorn Root: Protection; love and to keep a partner faithful
Valerian: Love; protection; purification and to calm nerves and relax muscles
Vanilla: Love; lust; luck; insight; aphrodisiac; used to increase power of potions
Venus Flytrap: Love and protection
Vervain: Love and fidelity; courage; peace and protection
Vetch (Giant): Fidelity
Vetivert (Khus Khus): Love; luck; protection; exorcism and peaceful harmony
Violet: Love; aphrodisiac; to get what you want
Walnut: Fertility
Wheat (Wheatgrass): Fertility
White Pepper: Aphrodisiac
White Willow Bark: Love; divination and protection
Wild Cherry Bark: Love and divination
Willowherb (Chamaenerion Angustifolium): To turn authoritarianism to humanitarianism
White Sage: Purification
Willow: Love; divination; protection and conjuring
Winter's Bark: Success
Wintergreen: Luck; strength; protection and to break hexes
Wisteria: Anointing; meditation; channeling; mental concentration and feminine sexuality
Witch Hazel Bark: Love; fidelity and to heal broken hearts

Wolf's Bane (Aconitum or Monk's Hood): Protection and invisibility (Deadly poison: Do not ingest.)
Witches Burr: To destroy evil and to add power to any formula
Wood Betony: Love and protection
Wood Rose: Good luck; imparts occult powers to the possessor
Woodruff: Money; protection and success
Wormwood: Love; protection; to call spirits and to cause trouble and strife for enemies
Yarrow: Divination regarding love; courage and exorcism
Yellow Evening Primrose (Primula Vulgaris): A successful hunt
Yellow Poplar Leaves: Love and binding
Yerba Mate: Love; lust and fidelity
Yerba Santa: Beauty; psychic powers and protection
Ylang Ylang: Insight; past lives and lust
Yohimbe: Love and lust
Zedoary: Protection; purification; courage; aphrodisiac and to break hexes
Zinnia: Love; energy; strength and mental balance

Minerals

Alabaster: Drawing and attracting
Amethyst: Love and peace
Black Tourmaline: To keep your love life in order
Carnelian: Passion; lust and courage
Clear Quartz: Neutral power
Coral: To attract love and affection; to enhance self-esteem
Diamond: To create a deeper bond; trust; love
Emerald: Love; heals the heart
Garnet: Love; lust; passion and courage
Green Moss Agate: Love; emotional strength
Hematite: Clear thinking and emotional stability
Iolite: Love; spiritual love; compassion and happiness
Jade: Love; success; joy; peace and abundance
Kunzite: Love; harmony and peace
Lodestone: Drawing; attracting; magnetization

Moonstone: To fall in love; for happy relationships; to protect women and for flashes of insight

Opal: To attract love

Pink and Watermelon Tourmaline: Love; passion; friendship and fulfillment

Red Jasper: Love and passion

Rhodochrosite: To heal the heart and to attract emotional and sexual love

Rose Quartz: Love; romance; friendship and emotional healing

Ruby: Love and passion

Star Sapphire: Protection from unfaithful lovers

CHAPTER 5
LOVE POTIONS

Many of the potions listed in the formulary below can be purchased from metaphysical shops, however, you can easily make them yourself. Because you have control over the quality and quantity of the ingredients and they are charged with your own energy and intentions, these potions are likely to be far more powerful than any you can purchase.

Use the same timing for potion-making as you would for spell casting based on your purpose. For example, potions to attract love may bring better results when they are created during a waxing or full moon. Friday is a good day to make such potions, but try to avoid making them on Saturday or when the moon is waning.

To make a powder from any of these, combine and pulverize the herbs listed in the recipe in dried form using a coarse mortar and pestle or an inexpensive coffee grinder.

Powders formulas may be burned as incense. Typically, incense formulas do not need to be ground as finely a powders.

You can produce an oil in two ways:

(1) Combine the dried, powdered form of the herb with a

base oil, such as Almond, Safflower or Sunflower. Cover the herbs with oil in a glass jar completely, then about two times more so that 1/2 to 1/3 of the jar is comprised of herbs and the other 1/2 to 2/3 is comprised of oil. Allow this to sit for, at least, two weeks in a warm place. Shake the jar twice per day. Then, strain the oil into a bottle using cheesecloth or a strainer and label it accordingly.

(2) Combine a few drops of each essential oil of the herb in the recipe into a base of about a cup of Almond, Safflower or Sunflower oil.

To create a house wash using any of these recipes, combine the herbs and boil them, strain and use the liquid as a wash to scrub the floors, walls, porch and sidewalk of your home or business.

To make a ritual bath, place several drops of oil in a bath.

To make a wash suitable for body or bath, combine the oil with unscented Castille soap. Dilute this soap to make the wash suitable for virtually any surface that can be cleaned.

To make bath salts combine sea salt with powder or oil and crush it using a mortar and pestle.

Store your formulas in jars with airtight lids away from heat and light. Label and date each one as you complete it.

Powders may be sprinkled around your place or business and used in mojo bags, which are, also, called charm bags or medicine bags and constructed as talismans.

Oils may be applied to your clothes or to mojo bags and used to strengthen your other spells.

Take care applying certain oils to your skin, particularly if you are sensitive or prone to allergies. For example, Cinnamon oil may burn your skin if it is not well-diluted with a carrier oil. If you are pregnant or nursing, you should take care not to apply these oils to your skin. Essential oils should never be used on infants or cats. Never ingest these formulas.

As you create these formulas, meditate on their purpose. Ask for spirit guidance and use your intuition. If you want to use a little more of one powder or oil in your formula, that's fine. If you feel the formula could benefit from a pinch of another ingredient according to the information provided in *Chapter 4*, follow your intuition.

Abbreviation Key for Measurements

T. = Tablespoon
tsp. = teaspoon
oz. = ounce
g = gram
ml = milliliter

Conversion of Measurements

3 tsp. = 1 T.
1 cup = 16 T.
1 cup = 8 oz.
1 pint =16 oz.
1 pint = 2 cups
1 tsp. = approximately 4.2 g
1 cup liquid = approximately 220 to 240 g
1 cup non-liquid = approximately 120 to 140 g
1 dram = 1/8 oz. = 60 grams = 3.697 ml = 60 drops
1 dram = .125 fl. oz. or approximately 3/4 tsp.
1 pint = approximately 473 ml
1 ml = 15 drops of liquid

Love Oils

The following oils may be worn on clothes, used to dress candles, mojo bags or other magical articles and worn on the skin. These oils should be kept away from eyes and membranes and never taken internally. Some people may be sensitive or allergic to an ingredient, in these cases the oil should not be applied to the skin.

These formulas should never be applied to infants or pets. Pregnant women should take special caution with some herbs and their volatile oils.

Admiration Oil

Wear this oil not only to attract romantic admiration, but to garner the approval of others.

1 /2 cup Almond oil
7 drops Jasmine oil
3 drops Ylang-ylang oil
3 drops Rose oil
3 drops Cowslip oil

Blend these ingredients together in a bottle and leave them in the moonlight.

Attract a Woman Oil

1 cup Almond oil
3 drops Allspice oil
6 drops Ambergris oil
6 drops Ambrette oil
3 drops Carnation oil
6 drops Cinnamon oil
3 drops Patchouli oil

Attraction Oil

1/2 cup Almond oil
7 drops Rose oil
3 drops Lavender oil
3 drops Vanilla oil
3 drops Sandalwood oil

Blend these ingredients together in a bottle and leave them in the moonlight. Apply this oil in the presence of the one you want to attract to you.

Banishing Oil
To drive away unwholesome energies
or unwanted persons

1/4 cup Almond oil
5 drops Cedar oil
3 drops Clove oil
3 drops Dragon's Blood oil
8 drops Patchouli
Small piece of Jet or Black Obsidian in the master bottle.

Bend Over Oil
To dominate another person

Almond oil
Allspice
Bergamot
Calamus root
Cinnamon
Licorice root

Combine equal parts of the above dried herbs in a jar with a lid, cover them twice over with Almond oil. Keep it in a warm place for two weeks, shaking it once or twice per day. Then, strain and bottle it. For extra power add a few drops of Bergamot and Vanilla oils.

Come to Me Oil

1/2 cup Almond oil
3 drops Bergamot oil
7 drops Damiana oil
3 drops Jasmine oil
3 drops Rose oil

Come to Me Now Oil

1/2 cup Almond oil
3 drops Cinnamon oil
3 Drops Ambergris oil
2 Drops Ylang-ylang oil
2 Drops Vanilla oil
A pinch of Orris Root Powder

Controlling Oil
To make another person obey you

1 1/2 cup Almond or Safflower oil
1/3 cup Cascara Sagrada
1/3 cup Devil's Shoestring
5 drops Bergamot oil

Pulverize the dried ingredients and combine them in the base oil in a jar with a lid. Shake it twice per day for two weeks. Then, strain the liquid. Finally, add the Bergamot oil.

Follow Me Boy Oil No. 1

1 cup Almond oil
16 drops Calamus root oil
15 drops Catnip oil
15 drops Damiana oil
7 drops Frankincense oil
3 drops Honeysuckle oil
3 drops Vetivert oil
3 drops Vanilla oil

Follow Me Boy Oil No. 2

1 cup Almond oil
1 T. Orris root
1 T. Catnip
1 T. Calamus
1 T. Damiana
1 T. Jasmine
1 T. Licorice

Macerate the dried herbs in oil for, at least, two weeks. Strain and bottle. Optionally, add several drops of Neroli oil.

Follow Me Girl Oil

2 cups Almond oil
1/8 cup Birth Root
1/8 cup Calamus root
1/8 cup Cubeb
1/8 cup Damiana
1/8 cup Ginger
1/8 cup Sampson Snake root
1/8 cup High John the Conqueror root
High John the Conqueror or Calamus root
A few hairs from a loyal pet, preferably your own
9 drops Ambrette oil

Combine equal parts of the above herbs and allow them to macerate in oil for, at least, two weeks. Afterward, strain the liquid. Place a whole root of High John the Conqueror or Calamus in the master bottle. Finally, add a few pet hairs and the Ambrette oil.

Intranquility Oil
*To summon the Intranquil Spirit and
to encourage a lover to return*

1 cup Sunflower oil
5 drops Coconut oil
3 drops Lavender oil
2 drops Violet oil or the tops of 2 or 3 blossoms
Pinch of Black Pepper
2 drops Ginseng extract
3 drops of Allspice oil
Pinch of Knotweed
Pinch of Stinging Nettles

Jezebel Oil
Do as I say

1/2 cup Almond oil
2 tsp. Calamus
1 tsp. Catnip
2 tsp. Jezebel root
2 tsp. Lavender
2 tsp. Red Rose buds
2 tsp. Rosemary

Love Binding Oil

1/2 cup Almond oil
Cinnamon
Clove
Grape Leaves
Pink Sheets upon which you have slept with your beloved
Rose petals
Verbena leaves

Pulverize a pinch of each of these ingredients and combine them in the oil for, two weeks. Afterward, strain the liquid and bottle it. Wear a dab of this oil the next time you see your beloved.

Love Drawing Oil No. 1

1 cup Almond oil
3 drops Palma Rosa
5 drops Ylang-ylang
1 drop Ginger
3 drops Jasmine
2 drops Rosemary
5 drops Patchouli
3 drops Vanilla oil

Love Attraction Oil No. 1

1/2 cup Almond oil
3 drops Anise oil
2 drops Cinnamon oil (Omit if you have sensitive skin)
3 drops Clove oil
3 drops Sassafras oil

For use by a man, add a whole High John the Conqueror root to the bottle. For use by a woman, add a whole Orris root.

Love Attraction Oil No. 2

1/2 cup Almond oil
5 drops Patchouli oil
1 drop Cinnamon oil
1 drop Rosemary oil
1 drop Rose oil

Love Oil

1/2 cup Almond oil
3 drops Rose oil
3 drops Jasmine oil
3 drops Patchouli oil
7 drops Dragon's Blood oil
3 Red or Pink Rose buds
Small Rose Quartz in the master bottle

Lover Return Oil

1 cup Almond or Safflower oil
7 drops Rose oil or Rose Geranium oil
7 drops Jasmine oil
7 drops Gardenia oil
7 drops Violet oil or 3 or 4 violet blossoms
1 tablespoon Catnip, dried and powdered
Orris Root (optional)

Use the Orris root for potions intended to be used by a woman.

Lust and Seduction Oil

1/2 cup Almond oil
3 drops Ambergris oil
3 drops Sandalwood oil
3 drops Frankincense oil
3 drops Patchouli Oil
Pinch of Deer's Tongue powder
Orris or High John the Conqueror root

Wear this oil to inspire lust and seduce another person. If the potion is to be used by a woman, add a whole Orris root to the master bottle. If it is to be used by a man, add a whole High John the Conqueror root.

Separation Oil
For use in break up spells

1 cup Almond oil
2 T. Chili Powder
1 T. Cinnamon
2 T. Galangal (Low John)
2 T. Black Pepper
2 T. Iron Filings
2 T. Vetivert

Add nettles to this formula to make it sting! Further enhance its power by adding a broken necklace chain.

Sexual Power Oil
To attract sexual partners

1/2 cup Almond oil
1 drop Cardamom oil
3 drops Dragon's Blood oil
3 drops Ginger oil
3 drops Patchouli oil
3 drops Sandalwood oil

Love Powders

Use these formulas in spells, as sprinkling powders or in mojo bags. For greater ease of sprinkling, you may thin the mixture with corn starch or rice flour.

Aphrodisiac Powder

Combine equal parts of the following:

Bergamot
Cinnamon
Clove
Ginseng
Tamarind

Bend Over Powder
To dominate another person

Allspice
Bergamot
Calamus root
Cinnamon
Licorice roct

Domination Powder

Mix and pulverize equal parts of the following:

Bergamot
Calamus
Licorice Root

Fast Love Powder

1/4 cup Corn Starch
3 T. Cinnamon
2 T. Roses
Pinch of Lilac petals
1 tsp. Sugar

Fertility Powder
For women who desire greater fertility

Cinnamon
Patchouli
Myrtle
Sage
Vetivert

The most propitious time to make this formula is when the Moon is in Cancer. Sprinkle this powder in your bed, use it in fertility spells and meditations and dust your body with it.

Fidelity Powder

1 tsp. Allspice
3 tsp. Cloves
1 tsp. Deer's tongue
1/2 tsp. Mullein
1/2 tsp. White Sage
Pinch of Used White Bed Sheet Ashes

Follow Me Boy Powder

Mix and pulverize equal parts of the following:

Calamus root
Catnip
Damiana
Frankincense
Vetivert

Follow Me Girl Powder

Birth Root
Calamus root
Cubeb
Damiana
Ginger
Sampson Snake root
High John the Conqueror root
Ambrette oil

Combine equal parts of dried powdered Birth Root, Calamus, Cubeb, Damiana, Ginger, Sampson Snake, and High John the Conqueror. Mix and pulverize these ingredients. Add several drops of Ambrette oil and mix it thoroughly into the powder.

Love and Caring Powder

1 tsp. Gardenia
1 tsp. Lilac
1 tsp. Lily of the Valley
1 tsp. Lily

Love Powder
Love and meditation

1/2 oz. Peony
1/2 oz. Violet
1/2 oz. Lily of the Valley
1/2 oz. Red Rose leaves
3 oz. Orris root
3/4 tsp. of Benzoic Acid (or Benzoin oil)
1 1/2 tsp. Mace
5 drops Almond oil
10 drops Cinnamon oil

This formula is based on an old 19th Century Lavender Powder by Joseph A. Begy.[1] Combine dried powdered, dried ingredients first and mix them well. Blend the oils separately. Add the blended oils to the powdered mixture.

Love Powder No. 2
To attract a man

1 part Bachelor's Buttons
1 part Clary Sage
1 part Lavender
Pinch of Sassafras leaf
Pinch of Valerian

Lover's Delight Powder
To release inhibitions

Mix and pulverize equal parts of the following:

Sandalwood resin
Saw Palmetto
Quina Roja
Red Rose petals

Love & Lust Powder

Mix and pulverize equal parts of the following:

Apple Blossom
Lavender
Roses
Violet
Yarrow

Lust Powder

Mix and pulverize equal parts of the following:

Deer's Tongue
Galangal root (Low John)
Patchouli
Periwinkle

Separation Powder
For use in break up spells

2 T. Chili Powder
1 T. Cinnamon
1 T. Low John root (Galangal root)
2 T. Black Pepper
1 T. Iron Filings
1 T. Vetivert

True Love Powder

Mix and pulverize equal parts of the following:

Elecampane
Mistletoe
Verbena

Love Incense

These formulas are for very pure, loose incense, which is either burned as is or on a charcoal disc such as those sold at metaphysical stores. The advantage of using loose incense without charcoal is that the smoke it produces is very pure and untainted by fumes or harsh odors. The disadvantage is that it must be relighted frequently.

The easiest, most natural and pure method of using incense is simply as dried, crushed herbs and resins. When you use the formulas in this way, it is not necessary to grind them to an extremely fine powder. Essential oils may be added to them and they may be tossed onto a small flame in your fireplace or gathered in a safe incense burner and lit with a match or lighter. The Love Powder formulas above may, also, be converted for use as incense.

General Instructions: Grind and mix all of the ingredients together. Store in a cool place inside a glass jar with a tight lid. To use the incense, place one or two teaspoons into a thurible on a heat-resistant surface.

Special Word of Caution: It cannot be over-emphasized to the novice that charcoal discs become remarkably hot. Always use a metal burner and place it on a marble, brick, ceramic tile or other heat-resistant, non-flammable surface.

These formulas are provided for you to use solely on your own responsibility. When you burn incense, you should always take the precaution of having adequate ventilation and a fire extinguisher nearby. Do not burn incense in the presence of people who suffer from respiratory problems.

Aphrodisiac Incense

Mix and pulverize equal parts of the following:

Ambrette or Amber resin
Jasmine
Orange
Rose
Sandalwood

Attract a Dominant Lover Incense

1 part Safflower
1 part Sampson Snake root

Domination Incense

3 T. Clove
1 T. Calamus root
1 T. Dragon's Blood resin
1 T. Frankincense
2 tsp. Damiana
7 drops Bergamot oil

Fidelity Incense

Mix and pulverize equal parts of the following:

Dried Lime peel
Dried Orange peel
Magnolia
Orris Root
Rosemary
Skullcap

Love Attraction Incense

1 tsp. Cinnamon powder
1 tsp. Rosemary
1 tsp. Orris root
1/2 tsp. Yarrow powder
1/2 tsp. Ginger powder
Several Rose petals

True Love Incense
To attract a pure and long-lasting love

2 T. Copal resin
2 T. Damiana
1 tsp. Cinnamon

Inks of Art for Use in Love Spells

In any spell where you are required to write a request or make a sigil, you may use inks of art and write with a calligraphy pen or shaped quill.

In these formulas, Gum Arabic (sometimes called Acacia Gum) is used as a thickening agent. It is substance extracted from the the particular species of Acacia tree called Acacia Senegal.

Always powder the ingredients used in the creation of your inks very finely. Macerate and blend the formula until it is smooth. Adjust the thickness by the amount of Gum Arabic used. It can be thinned with a formula of 2 parts water and 1 part alcohol. Always, begin with a very tiny amount before adding more to avoid over thickening the ink.

Dove's Blood Ink
To attract love

2/3 ounce of Water
1/3 ounce of Alcohol
Dash of Gum Arabic
Dash Dragon's Blood resin
3 drops Rose Geranium
A few drops of Red Food Dye

Dragon's Blood Ink
To add power to any spells

2/3 ounce of Water
1/3 ounce of Alcohol
Dash of Gum Arabic
Dash of Dragon's Blood resin
A few drops of Red Food Dye

Bat's Blood Ink
To bind or curse

2/3 ounce of Water
1/3 ounce of Alcohol
Dash of Gum Arabic
Dash of Myrrh resin
Dash of Cinnamon
Add a few drops of Black Food Dye (Add a little Red Dye to make it a dark shade of red.)

Instructions:

Excluding the dye, combine the ingredients in a bottle and allow the resin to dissolve a little bit. Blend it in a mortar and pestle until it is smooth. Then, add the dye.

When creating inks or any other dyed potions, use a stainless steel vessel or one made of a kind of material that won't become stained by this process. Combine all other ingredients in the potion and mix them thoroughly before adding the dye to a smaller portion. Dye a small amount first, then continue adding dye until the ink is a color you are pleased with.

Carefully pour the freshly made ink into a short bottle or very small jar with a tightly fitting lid. Cap the bottle tightly and store it in a cool, dark place until you're ready to use it.

Always take care not to get ink on your clothes, carpeting or other surfaces that could be damaged.

Traditionally, blood alone is used as ink or added to ink for potency. Of course, a simpler alternative is to use a red ink pen for your love spells.

Angela Kaelin

CHAPTER 6
GLAMOUR SPELLS

Everyone feels more attractive when they look and feel their best. Use these spells and potions to make yourself more attractive and to enhance the effects of your other spells for love.

Apollo's Glory Hair Potion

If you are a man or woman whose hair is dry, brittle or thinning, use this potion daily for luxuriously thick and healthy hair. It may be more potent if made during a waxing moon or on a Thursday.

1 cup Coconut oil
1 T. Castor oil
10 drops Rosemary oil
10 drops Borage oil
10 drops Sage oil

After you have mixed the potion, hold the bottle in your hands and charge it. Then, recite the following incantation to Apollo, the sister of Artemis who is the youthful, athletic ideal of masculine beauty and a god of medicine and enlightenment:

"O, Apollo, god of beauty
whose glory is like the golden rays of the sun,
On this day, in this hour,
Bless this potion with your healing power."

For men with coarser hair, this oil works as a styling pomade. For men and women, this potion may be used as a hot oil treatment or applied to the hair overnight and washed out in the morning. Rinse with vinegar to remove the oil. It, also, works well as a beauty oil for those with dry or mature skin.

If you are experiencing dandruff add three drops of Tea Tree oil to this potion. Furthermore, if you are experiencing either dandruff or hair loss, examine the shampoo you are using. Choose an organic shampoo like Burt's Bees or use liquid Castille soap. Alternatively, make a strong tea of Soapwort, which is a natural herb used as a shampoo.

Spell to Make Yourself More Beautiful

Use this spell to enhance your beauty.

You will need the following:

Pink candle
Rose Water (formula below) or Rose oil and Almond oil

Light a pink candle and anoint yourself with Rose Water or several drops or Rose oil in 1/4 cup of Almond oil while reciting Ezekiel 16:13-14 as follows:

"Thus wast thou decked with gold and silver; and thy raiment was of fine linen, and silk, and broidered work; thou didst eat fine flour, and honey, and oil; and thou wast exceeding beautiful, and thou didst prosper into a kingdom."

"And thy renown went forth among the heathen for thy beauty: for it was perfect through my comeliness, which I had put upon thee, saith the Lord God."

Meditate on your ideal appearance for a few minutes. Leave the candle to burn for an hour or so before snuffing it out. Repeat this procedure for nine consecutive nights.

Rose Water

Rose Water is a classic formula for beauty and for attracting love. As a tonic, apply Rose Water directly to your skin for a lovely complexion. Add it to love potions and beauty cremes.

Rose water is created through a process of distillation in which steam is created by boiling Rose petals and collecting the moisture in a receptacle.

You will need the following:

A stainless steel stock pot with a convex lid
A stainless steel bowl small enough to fit inside the stock pot with, at least, a 1" space around it
A brick
1 to 2 quarts of fresh Rose petals
Distilled Water
Ice cubes

Place the stock pot on the stove. Place the brick inside. Sprinkle the petals all around the brick, but not on top of it. Add enough water to cover the petals, but do not cover the surface of the brick. Place the bowl on top of the brick. Place the lid upside down, so that the curved side is facing downward into the pot.

Allow the pot to come to a boil. Place some ice on top of the concave surface of the lid. This helps to create more steam. Do not allow the pot to boil dry. Your final product should have the sweet smell of Roses. Use your Rose Water immediately. Keep any extra Rose Water refrigerated.

Bust Enhancement Spell and Potion

This potion is a topical ointment designed to increase and enhance the appearance of your bust. Make this potion on the night of a waxing moon.

1/4 cup Coconut oil
1 T. Wild Yam (Discorea Vulgaris or Discorea Villosa) extract
1 T. Fenugreek seed oil
1 T. Fennel oil

Combine the above ingredients and mix them thoroughly. Hold the bottle in your hands and charge it. Then, recite the following incantation to Artemis:

"O Artemis, beauteous and fair goddess of love, bless this potion with your special powers."

Once or twice per day, rub 1 tsp. of this potion into the soft parts of your inner thighs and upper arms.

Beauty Bath

Enjoy this relaxing, skin beautifying bath.

Obtain as many as you can of the following ingredients:

Aloe
Basil
Cowslip
Rose water
Rose petals
Milk
Coconut milk
Lettuce
Life Everlasting
Orange leaves
Vanilla extract

Add equal parts of these herbs to a muslin sachet and drop it into your comfortably warm bath. Add liquid ingredients directly to the bath. Then, light a pink or white candle and ask the Goddess of Love to bless you with love, abundance and anything else you desire.

Facial Rejuvenating Meditation

If you are experiencing signs of aging on your face, such as deepening smile and frown lines or a sagging jawline, use this technique. It is very effective for releasing the tension that is causing the sagging, unblocking the glands to function more effectively and smoothing the facial lines, sometimes in a matter of seconds. It combines the manipulation of life force energy and acupressure with self-hypnosis or autosuggestion. You will see long-term results, if you repeat it frequently, at least, once per day.

Channels of energy run throughout the body carrying life force. The focus for this meditation is on a dual channel that runs up the center front of the body. You may perform this meditation while standing, sitting or lying down. You should make yourself comfortable, but not so much so that you fall asleep.

Begin by gathering energy, much as you would if you were charging an object. Visualize a ball of ultra-violet electricity, popping, cracking and vibrating in the pit of your stomach, behind your navel. Allow this ball of energy to grow and strengthen before you release it throughout your body. See it filling your entire body and slowly streaming out of your finger tips.

An ultra-violet, healing energy is now radiating out of all of your fingers like the light from a laser. Using just your pinkies, lightly touch the base of your throat on either side of your laryngeal prominence, also known as your Adam's apple. Allowing only your pinkie fingers to lightly stroke this area, move your fingers up, energizing this channel until you reach your jawline.

Once your pinkies are resting at your jawline, move them out to the angle of your jaw. If you hold tension here, locate the joint. If you have a lot of stress held here, it may be painful. If so, gently press this area and allow this pain to be released. This is, also, stimulating the glands here and allowing them to function properly, which helps to keep your jawline and neck smooth.

After you have released this point, say the word, "Who,"

aloud. Feel your facial muscles relax completely and go into a very natural position. Often sagging and wrinkles are caused by an improper facial posture.

After you say the word, "Who," repeat the following statement in a low, monotonous, even tone of voice: "From now on, when ever I say the word, 'Who,' my face will automatically become more relaxed and youthful looking than ever before." This is a deepening suggestion that sets up a loop of increased relaxation and revitalization of your face every time you say it. Anytime throughout the day that you feel tension in your jaw or anywhere in your face, simply say the word, "Who," and your face will automatically relax.

Now, return your fingers to the base of your throat, once again. See and feel the laser-like energy coming out of your finger tips. Move your fingers up the front of your neck on either side of your Adam's apple, again. This time, continue until you reach the outer corners of your mouth. Pause and energize this spot for a few seconds, visualizing and feeling the energy flowing out of your fingertips and upward through this channel.

Then, continue moving your fingers upward until you reach the outside of your nose. There, on either side of each nostrils, pause and allow the energy to flow into this center for a few seconds before proceeding upward.

Move your fingers up to the inside of the bridge of your nose, near the inner corner of your eyes. Pause here and allow the energy to flow out of your fingers before moving the energy all the way up, smoothing out any frown lines along the way as you move to the top of your forehead.

You may repeat this entire procedure, including the deepening autosuggestion, again, if you like. You cannot overdo it, although once per session may be enough. If you do this before a mirror, you . may see an instant improvement in your jawline and the reduction of smile and frown lines.

After you have repeated this part, the meditation is complete. But, you must stimulate the flow of energy throughout the center of your body from the bottom up in two final steps. Firstly, grasp the web of each of your hands between the index finger and thumb and massage these areas for a few seconds. Secondly, stimulate the energy in your feet by grasping each of your toes, massaging and, finally, gently pulling on each of them.

Psychic Plastic Surgery

If you are dissatisfied with any part of your appearance, use a crystal wand to re-shape your face or body and remove lines or sags.

Obtain a crystal wand which is either a long solid piece of natural clear quartz crystal, an orgonite or chakra healing wand. A description of these wands and how to design and use a powerful orgonite wand is described in another book by this author entitled, *Magical Healing: How to Use Your Mind to Heal Yourself and Others*. A selenite wand, also, works very well.

This operation is best performed while you are lying down. You may hold a crystal in your free hand for added power. Selenite and apophyllite are both very good choices for their natural ability to align the chakra centers and reach other energetic planes or frequency ranges. If your concern is aging skin, choose a honey calcite or yellow jasper to impart a slightly golden tone to the laser light.

Then, take the crystal wand in your right hand and use it as a plastic surgeon would use a laser. Point it directly at your face and neck to erase lines and wrinkles. Mentally direct the energy flowing out of the wand to energize and tighten the skin.

If you are unhappy with your body, use the crystal wand to re-shape it the same way. When you have finished, imagine a re-shaping mask descending upon your face and body, energizing and reforming it to your ideal.

Perform psychic plastic surgery frequently and you will slowly begin to see results.

Beauty Spell with Facial Mask

The following potion imparts a healthy glow to skin and helps to remove bacteria and waste from pores. Begin using it nightly for about a week prior to a big event for which you want to look your best.

1/2 cup Bentonite Clay
1/8 cup Turmeric powder
1/8 cup Kelp powder
1/8 cup Apple Cider Vinegar
7 drops Geranium oil
7 drops Rose oil
Pure water

Combine the Bentonite Clay, Turmeric and Kelp in a jar with a lid. Add vinegar and then enough water to create a spreadable texture. Mix until it is free of lumps. Then, blend in the essential oils and mix them thoroughly.

Apply this mask to your face using gentle upward strokes and avoiding the delicate eye area.

This mask will remain fresh as long as it is stored in an airtight jar.

Caution: Turmeric is a natural golden dye, so take caution with linoleum, other porous surfaces, towels and wash cloths to prevent staining. If your skin is very sensitive, reduce the amount of vinegar in this formula and replace it with water.

Mirror Beauty Spell

Use this spell to turn back time and create a more desirable and youthful appearance.

You will need the following:

Pink candle
Photograph of yourself
Needle or thorn with which to make an inscription
Mirror
Piece of adhesive tape
3 drops Geranium oil
3 drops Rose oil
3 drops Lavender oil

Choose a photograph of yourself in which you feel you look your best. The photo you choose doesn't have to be recent, it may be an older one, but it should be one that you like and you should be alone in the photo without the influence of other people around you.

Affix the photograph to the mirror using a piece of tape.

Inscribe your name on the candle three times. Anoint it with three drops each of Geranium, Rose and Lavender oils. Then, light the candle and turn out the lights so that you see your reflection in the mirror next to the photograph only by candlelight.

Hecate is the Greek goddess of death and rebirth, who is capable of regenerating and revitalizing herself and those who call upon her powers. Ask her to help you transform yourself to look like the image in your photograph.

"O, Holy Hecate, Queen of the Night,
As you restored Persephone from the darkness of Hades,
Restore me to a state of heightened health, beauty and vitality.
O, Holy Hecate, Queen of the Night,
Use your knowledge and power to restore my body, mind and spirit."

As you say these words, gaze into the mirror and see yourself becoming more vital and beautiful. Meditate on your own image for a few minutes before snuffing out the candle. Light the candle and repeat this incantation and meditation each night until you achieve the desired results.

Youth Tea

To stay young and attractive, drink the following as a tea or decoction:

2 cups Water
2 T. Pine Needles
1 T. Goji berries
2 T. Sage
1 T. Thyme
1 tsp. Life Everlasting flowers

Angela Kaelin

CHAPTER 7
SPELLS TO FIND AN UNKNOWN LOVE

These spells are designed to help you get a glimpse into the future or to send out vibrations into the cosmos to help you attract the love of your dreams.

To Attract a Man or Woman with Specific Qualities

You will need the following:

White or red candle
Piece of paper
Love Attraction Oil

Acquire a white or red candle. White is for purity and new beginnings; red is for passion. The candle may be a pillar, taper, 7-day candle or a man or woman figure candle

In a case where you are interested in more of a sexual relationship, you may prefer to use a genitalia candle. These are available at many botanicas and metaphysical stores.

Do some soul searching about what your ideal mate would be like. Then, on a clean piece of paper list each of the qualities you desire. At the bottom of the paper, add the words, "This is my true love. Bring him (or her) to me." Anoint the edges of the paper you've written on with a few drops of Love Attraction Oil.

If you are using a candle with a soft wax bottom, carve out a space in the bottom. Place the paper inside the space and place the candle in its holder. If you are using another type of candle, fold your paper once or twice and place it beneath the candle.

Light the candle and sit quietly meditating on your wish for this love. Concentrate on the flame and see it sending the message you wrote on the paper out into the universe. Allow the candle to burn out. Or, let it burn for a little while before snuffing it out over the course of three consecutive nights.

When the candle is completely burned down, place the refuse in a bag and bury it in your back yard or hide somewhere where it won't be found or thought of again for a long time.

Unicorn Spell to Attract Pure Love

The unicorn represents purity. Use this spell to attract a very pure love.

You will need the following:

Unicorn pendant or charm on a chain
Rose quartz
Rose oil

Anoint the unicorn pendant and the rose quartz with Rose oil. Place the pendant on a chain around your neck. Then, hold the rose quartz in your hand while imagining the kind of person you want to attract. Place the quartz in your pocket or in a love drawing mojo bag and keep it with you. At night place the unicorn and the quartz under your pillow. Do this until the love you desire arrives.

Goddess of Love Ritual Bath

Combine the following:

1/2 ounce Almond oil
3 drops Cypress oil
3 drops Rose oil
3 drops Vanilla oil

Add a few drops to a bath while meditating on attracting the love of your dreams. Afterward, dry off and anoint your body with this oil.

Ritual Love Drawing Bath

Use this ritual bath to draw the love you desire.

You will need the following:

Rose petal tea or Rose Water (formula in *Chapter 6*)
Vinegar
A cleaning cloth
Pink sheets with which to cover mirrors in your bathroom
White votive candle
Red votive candle
Pink votive candle
Rose oil
Sea Salt

Make a tea of rose petals and let it cool. Add a few drops of vinegar to it. Then, with a clean white cloth clean every surface in your bathroom.

Cover the mirrors with pink sheets. Light the votive candles and place them around your bathtub. Add several drops of Rose oil and half a cup of sea salt to your bath water.

As you bathe, envision the kind of love you want to have in your life.

When you are finished with your bath, step out of the tub

and dry off. Say, "I am now cleansed of my old vibrations. Now, I attract only love and the love I desire comes to me freely."

To Draw Your Soul Mate

Many people believe that every soul has a mate. This is a person with whom you may have shared many past lives. If you are seeking your soul mate, work this spell. It is best performed on a Sunday during a full moon.

You will need the following:

Red mojo bag
Copal
Thyme
Piece of paper

On a clean piece of white paper, write a message to your soul mate. Search your heart. Tell him or her that you are ready for them to come into your life and anything else you feel.

Fold the paper in half toward you.

Burn Copal resin and dried Thyme as an incense and pass the paper through the smoke while reciting the following incantation:

"My one true love,
where e're you may be.
Now make your way
Right here to me."

"Come here my love,
Come now to me.
Goddess of Love,
Smile upon me."

Do this three times. Focus all your energy on drawing your soul mate to you as you do this.

Place a pinch of dried Copal resin and dried Thyme into a cloth bag. Add your note. Keep it with you at all times for the next nine days consecutively.

On the ninth day, again, burn Copal and Thyme as incense. Pass the note through the smoke and recite the incantation three times. This time, burn the note.

To See Your Future Husband: The Dumb Supper

The dumb supper is an old method practiced in the Ozark Mountain region of Missouri and Arkansas intended to summon the spirit of a girl's future husband. It involves cooking a small meal and preparing a dining table for unseen guests. It is called a "dumb" supper because it is performed in complete silence.

Perform this operation in solemnity and silence between midnight and 3 o'clock in the morning. Dim or shut off all electric lights and light one or two candles on the dining room table. Alternatively, light the room with one or two old-fashioned oil lamps.

Prepare a meal that is as simple or complicated as you like. You may plan and serve a meal in three courses or serve the traditional Ozarks meal of sweet corn bread (recipe below).

As you prepare the meal, do every possible thing in reverse. Add ingredients to the bowl in reverse order and stir the batter in a counter-clockwise direction. If you are serving more than one course, serve dessert first, then the main course, followed by the appetizer. If you are working with a friend, take turns stirring, cooking or baking without uttering a sound.

Set the table with a plate, a set of silverware and napkins for every living person and for every anticipated spirit guest. If you are dining alone, set a plate for yourself and one for the spirit of your future husband.

Walk backwards as you distribute the plates, glasses, napkins, silverware, butter, salt and pepper shakers and condiments. If you are right-handed, set the table with your left hand and vice versa. Place forks on the right and knives and spoons on the left. Place glasses at the upper left corner of the plate.

Once the table is set and the meal is served, open the doors and windows. Then, sit at your own place at the table.

Bow your head reverently and silently call upon the spirits to bring your future husband to you.

The wind may begin to blow more intensely or you may hear dogs howling as the spirit approaches. If everything goes well, you will see the spirit of your future husband. This may occur any time during the course of the meal.

Sweet Corn Bread Recipe

Ingredients:

1 cup White Flour
1 cup Yellow Cornmeal
1/3 cup White Sugar
1/3 cup Brown Sugar
1 tsp. Sea Salt
3 1/2 tsp. Baking Powder
1 Egg
1 cup Milk
1/3 cup Olive, Grape seed or Sunflower Oil

Directions:

Preheat oven to 400 degrees F (200 degrees C). In a large bowl, combine the above dry ingredients and blend them. Then, stir in the egg, milk and oil. Blend this batter until it is free of large lumps. Pour it into a greased 11" x 7" baking dish.

Bake at 400 degrees for 20 to 25 minutes or until a toothpick inserted into the middle comes out clean. Cut it into little golden squares and serve with butter.

Erzulie Freda Spell to Attract a New Romance

The Erzulie are a family of spirits, called loa, in Haitian Vodou. Freda is a member of this family, who originated in Africa among the Yoruba-speaking people of Nigeria, where she was known as Oshun, the goddess of rivers. She is syncretized with Our Lady or Sorrows (Mater Dolorosa), which is another apparition of Mary among Catholics.

Erzulie Freda is said to work better for men than women, but as long as she is treated with respect, anyone can work well with her. She is a very beautiful and pampered spirit who enjoys beautiful, romantic and expensive gifts. Altars and items dedicated to her are very beautiful and decorated in pink, white and sometimes gold. Her symbol (veve) is a heart pierced with a vertical staff, with tendrils vining out from it on each side.

You will need the following:

Image of Erzulie Freda or Our Lady of Sorrows or a 7-day candle of either
Pink altar cloth
Pink or white candle
Glass of Champagne
Red Rose petals
Erzulie Freda Oil (formula below)
Love Incense (any you choose)
Any pink, feminine, lacy or frilly items you would like to add to the altar to honor her, including fresh flowers and jewelry
Piece of paper upon which to write a petition

Dress your altar with a pink cloth and place a glass of champagne by the image of Erzulie Freda. Sprinkle rose petals upon the altar and place any other offerings to her upon it.

Write out your request on the piece of paper, telling Erzulie Freda the exact nature of your desires. Then, anoint the candle with Erzulie Freda Oil. If you are using a 7-day candle, you will not need any other image of her or other candles.

Light the incense and the candle and call upon Papa Legba who is the key Vodou spirit, as follows:

"Papa Legba, please, cast aside the veil and allow me to speak to Erzulie Freda."

Pause reverently for a few moments before continuing, as follows:

"Erzulie Freda, I call upon you and ask that you be present with me here and now. I ask that you remove all obstacles that may lie between me and my love. Use your special powers to arrange things so that I may find the love that I desire and that I may [insert your petition]. Thank you for coming to me and honoring my request."

Close your prayers by saying:

"Papa Legba, thank you for allowing me to speak with Erzulie Freda. Please, close the veil."

Pass the petition paper through the smoke of the incense, fold it toward you and place it beneath the image or candle.

You may perform this spell in one night or repeat this procedure over the course of nine nights.

When the spell is complete, burn the petition paper and place the ashes and other refuse from this spell into a bag and bury it in your back yard.

Erzulie Freda Oil

1/4 cup Almond oil
1 T. Coconut oil
3 Basil leaves
Pinch of Red Rose petals
Vanilla bean

Combine the following ingredients into a bottle. It is not necessary to strain this oil before using it. Optionally, add a drop or two of Basil, Rose or Vanilla oil to strengthen this oil's potency.

Angela Kaelin

CHAPTER 8
SPELLS TO ATTRACT
A PARTICULAR PERSON

Cast these spells to make someone think or dream about you, to get them to call you, to turn friendship to love or create a bond with someone you desire.

Cast these spells to make someone think or dream about you, to get them to call you, to turn friendship to love and create a bond with someone you desire.

To Make Someone Call You No. 1

Use this spell to compel a prospective love interest to call you on the telephone.

You will need the following:

Piece of clean paper and a pen
New, unused sewing needle
Your telephone

On a clean, white piece of paper, write the name of your love nine times, end to end in an unbroken circle. As you do this, concentrate on the person's face and will them to call you. At the height of your concentration when you feel your energy is the highest, pierce the center of the circle with a new sewing needle.

Place the paper with the needle through it by your telephone.

Depending on how powerful your working was, you will receive a call within nine minutes, nine hours or nine days.

To Make Someone Call You No. 2
Wiccan Version

You will need the following:

Picture of the person
White candle
Your telephone

Cast a circle to purify the energies and strengthen this spell. Before you cast the circle, bring all of the items you will need into the center. Place a picture of your beloved by your telephone. Place a white candle directly in front of the picture.

Light the candle and intensely concentrate on the person calling you while you repeat the following incantation three times:

"By the power of three times three
Call me, my love. Call me."

Continue focusing your intention for the person to call you for a few moments until you feel that the spell has worked. Close the circle and wait for the call.

To Melt the Heart of Someone Who Has Rejected You

This is an ancient method of influencing a reluctant lover.

You will need the following:

Softened wax, preferably red
Personal effects
Needle or Nail
Fireplace or other safe place to build a small fire

Using soft warm wax, mold an effigy of the person. Fold personal effects such as a few hairs or nail clippings belonging to the person into the center of the effigy.

With a nail or a needle, inscribe his or her name upon the image. Then, allow it to melt over a fire while repeating the following incantation:

"As this wax melts, so melts the heart of [Name] for me."

Honey Pot Spell

Perform this spell whenever you want a friend or a acquaintance to behave more sweetly and generously toward you.

You will need the following:

Short, squat jar with a large mouth and a lid
Honey
Sweet syrup (corn syrup or pancake syrup)
Sugar
Needle or thorn with which to make an inscription
2 clean pieces of paper and a pen
Red, pink or white 7-day candle
Dandelion blossoms
Rose petals
Violet blossoms
Love Oil

Combine honey, syrup and sugar into the jar.

On a piece of clean white paper, write the name of the person you want influence nine times in a column. Then, turn the paper 90 degrees and write your own name over the top nine times.

Now, think for a moment about how you want the person to behave toward you. Then, write this request around the names in a circle, completely surrounding the names, without lifting your pen. Empower this spell by addressing your request to any deity, saint, angel or other spirits you want to help you.

Dip the edges of the paper in Love Oil. Sprinkle Violet blossoms on top of the paper. Place the second piece of paper on top of this.

Then, fold the papers in such a way that the blossoms stay in the middle, making all of the folds in a motion toward you. As you do so, name the person and state your intention aloud that the person should behave more sweetly toward you and whatever else you want from them.

Put the folded papers into the jar. Screw the lid down tightly.

Inscribe the person's name nine times in a spiraling fashion on the candle. Dress it with Love Oil. Place the candle securely on top of the jar. Use a little melted candle wax to keep it in place. Then, sprinkle Violet, Dandelion blossoms and Rose petals around the jar.

Let the candle burn out completely or let it burn for only an hour and then snuff it out. This spell can be done in one day or it can be drawn out over a period of several days or weeks by repeatedly speaking your petition and then burning the candle for about an hour and snuffing it out each day.

Put this jar and candle in a safe place so it won't catch anything on fire if it falls. Put it in your empty fire place or in a tub of rocks or sand. Make sure it is stable and in a place where it won't be disturbed by any commotion.

To Attract a Particular Lady

Do this spell over nine consecutive days beginning on a Tuesday.

You will need the following:

Red wax female figure candle
3 T. Honey or Sugar
A new, unused sewing needle.

With the needle, write the name of the lady you desire on the chest of the effigy candle. Apply a little honey to it or sprinkle it with sugar.

Then, light the candle and repeat the following incantation three times:

"Spirit, body and soul of [Name], through this candle, which I burn, you shall become weak and open to my will. My will shall overpower yours. You shall willingly become my consort."

Allow the candle to burn for half an hour or so while meditating on your purpose before snuffing it out. Perform the same operation again the next night at the same hour of the day. Do this for nine days.

At the end of this spell, if no wax residue remains, this is a good sign. If there is wax residue, continue to burn it until it is gone.

Tea to Inspire Someone to Love You

Brew and drink a cup of this tea for yourself on a Friday. Then, on the following Friday, brew it again and serve it to the object of your love. He or she will soon begin to fall in love with you.

Pinch of Rosemary
2 tsp. Green or Black Tea
3 pinches of Thyme
3 pinches of Nutmeg
3 Mint springs
6 Rose petals
6 Lemon leaves
3 cups Water
Sugar or Honey

While you brew and drink his tea, recite the following incantation over it:

"By the power of Circe, let it be that [Name] shall desire only me."

To Inspire Passionate Love

If you would like to inspire passionate love in someone, perform this spell on a cloudless night, approximately three nights before a full moon.

You will need the following:

Photograph of the person, something with their signature on it or other small, highly personal item
Red 7-day candle
2 White candles, small
Patchouli incense
Rose oil
Sea Salt
Water
Large bowl
Fresh Red Rose

Place the photograph, signature or personal item under or in front of the red candle on your altar. Then, take a bath with a cup full of salt and several drops of Rose oil. As you bathe, clear your mind of any thoughts except your purpose in performing this spell. Imagine attracting passionate love from the person who is the subject of this spell.

After your bath, fill your bowl with the very pure water. Take the bowl, the Rose and Salt with you outside. Clear your mind again and focus on your goal.

Hold the bowl of water so it reflects the light of the moon toward you. Imagine pulling the energy of the moon into the water in a stream of light. Do this for a few minutes. When you feel that the water is fully charged, pour a palm full of salt into your hand and sprinkle it into the bowl in a clockwise circle.

As if you are speaking to the water, repeat the following incantation three times:

"I charge you to call forth the passionate love of [Name] for me."

Stir the salt in the bowl with the Rose in a clockwise motion. When it is dissolved, dip the Rose into the water and sprinkle the water on yourself from head to toe.

Return to your altar.

Light the two white candles and say:

"By the power of the full moon, [Name} will be here soon."

Light the red candle and say:

"Flame of passion I light thee, the passion of [Name] for only me.

Hold your hands out, with your palms palms facing the candles and pour into them all the energy you can conjure. When you feel this is done sufficiently, stop and light the incense.

"Draw [Name] near by thy smoke.
His (or her) passion for me conjure and stoke."

Allow the candles to burn down, all the while meditating upon your goal. When the candle has completely burned down say, "Amen" or "So mote it be!"

Instead of letting the candles burn down completely, you may divide this spell over the course of three nights. This powerful spell may begin to take effect before the red candle burns down completely.

To Attract Physical Love

Perform this spell when you want to attract a physical relationship.

You will need the following:

Red candle, medium to large pillar or 7-day
Love Attraction Oil
Lust Powder or Love and Lust Powder
Needle or thorn with which to make an inscription
Rue, dried
Photograph of the person
Lodestone and iron filings

Inscribe the person's name nine times onto the candle. Anoint it with Love Attraction Oil or a similar potion, while concentrating on your desire.

Light the candle.

Place some Rue in a sturdy incense burner and light it. Pass the photograph through the smoke, while repeating the phrase, "[Name], come to me and love me."

Place the photo on your altar in front of the candle. Sprinkle it with Lust Powder, Love and Lust Powder or some other suitable potion.

Place the lodestone on top of the photograph and feed the stone with a small amount of iron filings.

Meditate on your desires for a few minutes. Allow the candle to burn for about half an hour before snuffing it out.

Perform this operation for 15 days in a row while, thinking intently about making love to your beloved.

Old-fashioned Love Attraction Oil Lamp

Vintage kerosene lamps are an elegant and cost-effective alternative to candles and may be used on an altar in place of a candle or alone as a spell to draw love. The following spell to create a Love Attraction Oil Lamp is best begun on a Tuesday or Friday during a waxing moon.

You will need the following:

Old-fashioned kerosene or paraffin lamp
Vegetable-based lamp oil
2 Lodestones
Rose Quartz
Ginseng or Orris root
Vanilla bean
Personal effects, such as hair or nail clippings
Love Attraction Oil

Begin with a clean lamp and an empty oil compartment. As you add your Lodestones, small piece of Rose Quartz, root, bean and personal effects of your intended lover, concentrate on the purpose of each one. Add a few drops of Love Attraction Oil or a similar formula and then fill the rest of the chamber with a vegetable-based lamp oil, which is available at many department stores and online.

Charge the contents of the lamp and concentrate on your desires. Place the lamp on your altar alone or before the image of spirits you work with and invoke their assistance.

Tips for using an old-fashioned oil lamp:

Roll the wick up and trim each of the corners slightly to keep the glass chimney from becoming blackened. Then, roll it down so that only 1/4 to 1/2" appears at the mouth of the burner. If you have just installed a new wick, wait a few hours before lighting it so it has time to soak up the oil.

After you light the wick, adjust the size of the flame by

turning the knob on the side of the lamp. Then, place the chimney on top.

Always treat oil lamps with the same caution you would use with candles. Place them on a stable surface where they will not be disturbed and do not leave them unattended. Refill the reservoir with oil frequently. Do not allow the oil to burn away completely.

Hoodoo Love Attraction Oil Lamp

A very simple, beautiful style of natural oil lamp is commonly used in Hoodoo spells. Hoodoo oil lamps are powerful, economical substitutes for candles.

To attract the love of a particular person, create this elegant oil lamp on the night of a waxing moon.

You will need the following:

Orange, Grapefruit or Yam
Vegetable oil
Cinnamon bark
Orris root or Vanilla bean
Garnet, Moonstone or Rose Quartz
Personal effects
Love Attraction Oil
Wick or a slice of cork approximately 1/8" thick
Wick tab

Halve an Orange or Grapefruit and carefully remove the fruit while leaving the peeling in tact. Alternatively, create a hollow in the center of a large Yam by scooping out the center portion. This will be the reservoir for your oil and other items.

Add the herbs, gemstones and personal effects. Pour oil into the reservoir. Cut a short piece of wick and place it in the center of a wick tab or a slice of cork, which has been pierced in the center. Place the wick and the tab on the surface of the oil where it should float. Charge the lamp and impregnate this energy with your desires. Then, light the wick.

Another variation on Hoodoo vegetable oil lamps can be made using a glass or a heavy Pyrex vessel. Do not use globular shaped vessels like wine glasses, however, because they can easily break if the flame floats under the edge if the glass.

Place your herbs, stones, personal effects and drops of magical oil into the vessel. Add water up to approximately an inch from the top. Optionally, add a few drops of green or yellow food coloring. Pour a thick film of vegetable oil over the top of the water. Place a short piece of wick inserted through a wick tab on the surface. If the layer of oil on top of the water is thick enough, the wick and tab should float.

Customize your lamps based on your desire according to *Chapter 4. List of Love Herbs, Minerals and Their Properties.*

Always stabilize your Hoodoo oil lamps in a bed of sand or stones for fire safety. Use the lamps for long-term spells and novenas. Write out your request or petition on a piece of paper and place it under the lamp.

Angela Kaelin

CHAPTER 9
SPELLS TO BIND A LOVER TO YOU

Work these spells when you are in a relationship you want to strengthen.

Passion Tea

To increase the passion in your relationship:

3 to 4 cups Water
Handful of Rose petals
3 whole Cloves
1 Nutmeg
1 Cinnamon stick
1 tsp. Ginger, powdered or grated
Honey or Sugar to taste

Combine these ingredients to make a tea or decoction. Strain it and allow it to cool. Drink it together with your beloved.

Spell to Create a Jack Ball

This spell is for the creation of a Hoodoo device called the Jack Ball, which is employed to bind and control a lover and to divine his or her secrets. It is, also, used in the case of a staying or wandering lover depending on how you focus your intention during its construction. It is traditionally used to control a man, but it can easily be adapted to control a woman.

You will need the following:

Red yarn
Wax from a white paraffin or old-fashioned bee's wax candle
Personal effects such as hair, nails or bodily fluids from your lover
Needle with a large eye through which to thread a piece of yarn
Optionally, a whole High John the Conqueror Root and a drill or knife with which to make a whole in it

There are different ways to create a Jack Ball. In this first method, you will use a combination of warm wax and personal effects from your lover to form a ball, approximately 3/4" in diameter, although you can make it as large or small as you like. Once it is made, you will keep it with you at all times and not allow anyone else to touch it or know about it.

Begin by surreptitiously gathering hairs, nail clippings and bodily fluids from your beloved. Carefully, gather the soft wax of a melting candle and mix these personal effects into the middle of a wax ball. To this mixture you may add your own fluids, in particular, urine and menstrual blood to gain power over the person who is the target of the spell. As you are forming the ball, focus your thoughts on your purpose. You can even chant: "[Name], come and stay by me. Be true. Do as I say." Use whatever words best suit your purpose.

Once you have formed the ball, begin wrapping it in yarn just as you would wrap a ball of twine. Again, as you wrap, focus your thoughts on your purpose. When it is completely covered, clip the yarn leaving a long tail. Do not knot the yarn. Instead, thread the yarn through the needle and work the tail back through the center of the ball. This should leave you with a ball securely suspended from the end of this piece of yarn.

Cut another piece of yarn approximately twice the length of the tail. Thread one end through the end of the needle and run it through the the ball at the base of the tail. This will leave you with three strands of yarn dangling from the end of the ball. Braid these three strands to form one tail and secure the end of it with a knot.

Use this ball to gain control of your lover by commanding it and applying your urine or blood to it. Command it and dominate it with your words and thoughts.

Address the ball as if you were speaking to your lover and say, "[Name], come under my control."

To use a Jack Ball to gain control of a man and "cut" his masculine power, particularly his sexual prowess, cut or drill a whole High John the Conqueror root. Place the personal effects inside of it and seal the hole with wax. Wrap it with yarn, leaving a long tail for it, as previously described.

To know what your lover is doing or thinking, use this ball as a pendulum. Tune the Jack Ball pendulum by adjusting its length. A shorter length swings faster than a longer one. This is a matter of personal preference.

The pendulum works on the basis of energy and impulses sent through the body as a result of directed thought. Whenever you use a pendulum, you must formulate a question and then wait for the response with the attitude of an observer.

A pendulum does not work exactly the same way for every person. There are two ways to determine pendulum indications for you.

The first is to simply ask the pendulum. Hold the pendulum suspended in front of you and command it. Say, "Show me what 'yes' is for me." Then, wait and watch what the pendulum does. It may go in a clockwise or counter-clockwise circle, it may swing back and forth or it may remain still. This is your "Yes" indication.

Then, command it to show you your "No" response. Say, "Show me what 'No' is for me." Then, wait and watch what the pendulum does. This is your "No" indication.

The second method is to program the pendulum to move as you want it to for certain indications. A common is to have the pendulum swing back and forth for yes, from side to side for no and around in a circle when the question cannot be answered.

Make these pendulum motions intentionally, at first. Practice like this for a few minutes.

Then, pause and test your pendulum by asking it a question you already know the answer to. For example, "Is my name _____?" Then, wait for the answer.

Hold the pendulum over a common object like a book and ask, "Is this a book?" Wait for the answer. Then, hold the pendulum over the same object and as, "Is this a rock?"

After you do this several times and receive consistently correct responses from the pendulum, it is programmed.

Now, you can use this pendulum in this way to elicit "Yes" or "No" responses. Such as, "Is my lover cheating?"

Or, you can use it much as you would use a Ouija board. You can even use it in conjunction with the spirit board or draw out letters and numbers on a sheet of paper.

For example, if you believe your lover is cheating, ask the pendulum to tell you the name of the person. This process requires patience, but it can astonishingly effective. Start by determining the initials of the person. Go around the board from A to Z and ask, "Is the first initial of his or her name 'A?'" Then, wait for a response from the pendulum before moving to the next letter.

Love Potion No. 9

Serve this love philter to your lover to intensify your relationship. The origins of this spell are uncertain, but it appears to be very old. It contains wine and nine powerful love herbs.

Make it on ninth day of September at the ninth hour of the day.

As you make Love Potion No. 9, consider all of the ways you can incorporate the number "9" into its manufacture. Before you begin, light nine pink candles.

Then, combine the following in a pot on the stove:

9 cups sweet Red Wine (or Concord Grape juice)
9 Cinnamon sticks
9 Red Rose petals
9 Cloves
9 Apple seeds
9 Anise stars
9 drops Vanilla extract
9 pieces of Ginseng root
Juice from 9 Persimmons

Stir the potion nine times. Each time you stir it pronounce the following incantation:

"When [Name] drinks this wine,
He (or she) will shower me love divine.
Sweet Love Potion No. 9,
Make him (or her) forever mine."

Bring the potion to a boil, then reduce the heat and allow it to simmer for nine minutes. Then, remove it from the heat and allow it to cool.

Blow on the potion nine times while reciting the names of the following nine goddesses of love each time: Inanna, Ishtar, Astarte, Hathor, Nephthys, Aphrodite, Venus, Freya, Arianrhod.

Strain the liquid. Refrigerate it. Do not tell anyone about it or let anyone else see or touch it. Serve it to your intended lover within a day or two but do not tell him or her that it is a love potion, lest the effects be lessened or negated.

Santa Muerte Spell to Bind the Heart of a Lover

Santa Muerte is, also, called Saint Death or Holy Death. She is the Goddess of Death in Mexico and an extremely powerful, indulgent and protective maternal figure.

She is not recognized as a saint by the Catholic Church, but she is the mother of all. You can ask anything of her and she will grant it without making any moral judgments. For example, if you were in love with a married man or woman and wanted to destroy that person's marriage, she would give you what you desire and protect you from any consequences.

She may be called upon for any purpose whatsoever. Simply make your request. For example, you can can ask her to bring an end to your own unwanted relationship; stop unwanted attention, get rid of interference from others or strengthen and empower or current relationship. You can, also, ask for her assistance in strengthening any of your other spells.

She is very powerful, but she requires devotion. Therefore, if you decide to use her, give her a special place in your home with a devotional statue or other image and she will help you with anything else you need. Make a small sacrifice to her, address a prayer to her as "Most Holy Death" and make your request.

Santa Muerte gladly accepts cigarettes, alcohol, flowers and candy. Although, you may offer her anything you like as it comes from your heart. Lay it on the altar before the candle, which has her image on it, then ask for the cloak of her protection to be placed over you and your family.

In this spell, a request is made for Santa Muerte to bind a lover to you and keep him or her faithful.

You will need the following:

Image of Santa Muerte on a prayer card (or printed from the internet)
Red altar cloth
Red Apple
Container with a lid, large enough for the Apple to fit into
3 Red Roses
Photo of your beloved
Photo of yourself
Red candle
Love Binding Oil
Needle or thorn with which to make an inscription
2 to 3 feet of red ribbon, approximately 1/2" to 1" wide
6 feet of red yarn or ribbon
Black, fine pointed marker
Cinnamon powder
Honey

Inscribe your name and your lover's name on the candle. Anoint it with Love Binding Oil.

Dress your altar with a red cloth and place the candle on top of it.

With the marker, write the name of your beloved three times upon the ribbon. Then, write your name over the top three times with the marker. Write your petition to Santa Muerte on the remaining ribbon. Ask her to bind your lover to you and make him or her true.

Make seven knots in the ribbon while repeating the following prayer each time you cinch:

"Santa Muerte, tie [Name] to me. With this knot, we are bound together forever."

Using the ribbon, tie the photographs of yourself and your beloved together face to face. Place this on the altar in front of the candle. Place the image of Santa Muerte on top of the bound photographs.

Charge the candle and ask for Santa Muerte to come and be present with you.

"O Holy Death, I summon you to enlighten my home with your holy presence. I humbly ask that you grant me that which I most desire. Break and destroy and curses that may have been placed upon me and bless me with the love of [Name], that we may be bound together in loving harmony for all eternity. [Make your petition.] O Holy Death, you are my protector. Destroy all of my enemies, both great and small, and any who would harm me or those I love."

Light the candle and repeat your prayer and petition to Santa Muerte over the course of nine consecutive nights.

On the ninth night, when the candle is burned out completely, apply Honey to the ends of the ribbon and sprinkle them with Cinnamon powder

Cut the Apple in half. Place your photographs tied with the ribbon and the image of Santa Muerte in between the two halves of the Apple. Bind the Apple back together with a piece or red ribbon or yarn. Place it inside the jar along with the Roses. Drizzle Honey inside the jar. Finally, place the lid on the jar and tighten it. Then, bury it in your yard.

Love Strengthening Floor Wash

Increase the love vibrations in your home by washing the walls, floors and other hard surfaces of your home and your porch with this floor wash:

2 quarts Water
Petals from 3 Red Roses
1/3 cup dried Skullcap
1 tsp. Lemon oil
1 tsp. Vanilla extract

Boil the Rose petals and Skullcap in water for several minutes. Allow the mixture to cool. Strain it. Add the Lemon oil and Vanilla extract.

Aphrodisiac and Natural Lubricant

Combine the following essential oils in a jar and use this natural aphrodisiac and lubricant whenever it is needed.

4 T. Coconut oil (slightly warmed so it becomes liquid, but not hot)
4 T. Almond oil
7 drops Vanilla oil
7 drops Sandalwood oil

Spell to Keep an Unfaithful Man True

This is an old American Hoodoo spell to bind a man to you and make him true.

You will need the following:

Piece of string or yarn no more than a foot long
Piece of string or yarn long enough to tie around your waist
Red votive candle
Hairs collected from every part of your body
Pair of scissors or shears

Use the shorter string to measure the man's instrument of pleasure. This must be done secretly. Cut this string at the same length. At 9 o'clock in the evening, tie nine knots in the string. Tie this string to the longer piece of string and tie it around your waist. Undress and collect the hairs from your body with a pair of scissors

Light the red candle and burn the hairs on its flame with the desire for your man to love you and be true.[2]

St. Martha the Dominator Spell to Keep a Lover Faithful and Be Treated with Respect

St. Martha the Dominator is the sister of St. Lazarus and is, also, called St. Martha of Tarascon. She is sometimes confused with her cousin, St. Martha of Bethany. But, St Martha is know for the miracle of dominating the Tarasque, which was a dragon with the head of a lion, six short legs and the body of an ox with a stinging tail, covered in tough armor. According to legend, it lived in Provence in southern France. Knights had been sent to destroy the beast, but none could prevail until St. Martha charmed it with her prayers, Holy Water and Hyssop.

St. Martha's Feast Day is July 29th, her day is Tuesday and her colors are green, white and red. Her symbols are a torch, a dragon and a Holy Bible with a cross on its cover.

In serious cases, she is appealed to by means of a novena, which is a series of prayers conducted over the course of nine consecutive days or sometimes nine consecutive Tuesdays.

St. Martha the Dominator is usually appealed to in cases where a woman needs to dominate a situation involving a man, whether in love or business affairs. Although, she will work in situations where a woman must dominate another woman, if that woman is controlling or abusive. While St. Martha does work for men, they must be very pure and in a situation where they are truly victims in need of assistance.

On a Tuesday, perform this spell to keep your lover faithful and be treated with love and respect.

You will need the following:

Image of St. Martha or St. Martha 7-day candle
Red candle or a green or white candle tied with a red ribbon (unless you are using a St. Martha 7-day candle)
St. Martha Oil (formula below)
St Martha Incense (formula below)
Glass of Water
Sweet white wine or fresh flowers

Anoint the candle with St. Martha Oil while you recite the following prayer:

"St. Martha, I dedicate this candle to you.
I ask that you help me with all of my necessities
And help me to conquer my difficulties,
Just like you conquered the Tarasque."

Place the candle on your altar next to the image of St. Martha, if you are using one. Place a glass of water next to the image as an offering along with a small glass of white wine or a few fresh flowers.

Light the candle and burn a small amount of incense while you recite the following prayer:

"O, Holy St. Martha, you, who entered the mountain
And tamed the beast with your Hyssop and your prayers
And bound it with your ribbons and brought it under
your feet,
As you dominated the beast, I beg you to bind and
dominate [Name].
Let him have no peace, let him know no rest or comfort
Until he is humble and submissive at my feet.
O Holy St Martha, hear me and grant my desire. Amen."

You may continue this prayer over the course of nine consecutive days or nine consecutive Tuesdays.

St. Martha Oil

1/4 cup Almond oil
3 drops Dragon's Blood oil
3 drops Hyssop oil
3 drops Spikenard oil
Calamus root in the master bottle

St. Martha Incense

Calamus root
Dragon's Blood resin
French Tarragon
Hyssop blossoms
Holy Water

Combine equal parts of the above dried, powdered herbs. Sprinkle the mixture with a few drops of Holy Water.

Bella Marta Spell to Obtain a Marriage Proposal

Bella Marta is not St. Martha, but a forest nymph or dryad of the Tuscany region of Italy. Because she is a woodland spirit, you must go to a wooded area to make your first contact with her.

You will need a few hairs from the head of your beloved wrapped in a handkerchief. After midnight, you must go unseen into the most beautiful park or garden you have access to and kneel before the most beautiful, old tree in it.

Then, recite the following prayer:

"Beautiful Marta! Beautiful Marta! Beautiful Marta!
Thou art beautiful as a star.
I come to behold you once more,
Once more to kneel before you,
That I may adore you better.
Midnight has struck,
I am kneeling before you
Kneeling in a fair garden,
Where thou, beautiful Marta, art queen.
I bring thee a handkerchief;
Within it thou wilt find
The hairs of my beloved,
And thou, oh Marta, cause
What thou wilt that my trouble may pass to my good,
Cause him to marry me,
May he never love other women
Grant me this grace,
And thou shalt have
Every evening a lighted candle.
This thou wilt surely grant me,
Beautiful Marta, I thank thee!"[3]

Fold the handkerchief and place it deep into the knot of the tree or bury it near the roots. Then, return home without looking back. When Bella Marta grants your request, keep your promise to light a candle for her every evening or else she might withdraw the favor.

Angela Kaelin

Incantation to Marry in Grand Style

If you would like to marry and wish to do so stylishly, on the night of a waxing moon, light a red candle and recite the following incantation.

"Diana, beautiful Diana!
Thou who didst save from a dreadful death
When I did fall into the dark ravine!
I pray thee grant me still another grace.
Give me one glorious wedding, and with it
Full many bridesmaids, beautiful and grand;
And if this favour thou wilt grant to me,
True to the Witches' Gospel I will be!"[4]

Meditate on the wedding of your dreams for a few minutes. Allow the candle to burn for a little while before snuffing it out.

Light the candle and repeat this incantation with feeling over the course of nine consecutive nights.

Spell to Draw a Lover Closer and Stop Interference

Sometimes an otherwise happy couple will experience interference in their relationship from relatives or friends. In such a cases, the first thing you must do is draw your lover closer and reinforce his or her allegiance to you so that he or she will come to your defense whenever you or your relationship is being criticized by outsiders.

You will need the following:

2 Red candles, tapers or figure candles to represent you and your lover by gender
3 Small pieces of clean, white paper
Love and Caring Powder
Some Hairs from each of you
Bag or a small box

Cut three small pieces of paper approximately 4" by 4". Place them in a row in front of you.

On the first paper (the one on the left) write your name in the center of it and draw a circle around it.

On the second paper, (the middle one) write your name and your lover's name together in the center of it and draw a circle around both names together. On the third paper (the one on the right) write your lover's name in the center of it and draw a circle around it.

Place the candle representing you on top of your name on the first paper. Place the candle representing your lover on top of his or her name on the third paper.

Light the candle that represents yourself and say, "The flame of love burns strong and bright in the heart of [Your Name]."

Then, light the other candle and say, "The flame of love burns strong and bright in the heart of [Lover's Name]."

Sprinkle Love and Caring Powder or a similar Love Powder in the symbol for infinity (a figure "8") around the candles, crossing over at the point where both of your names are written in a circle.

Trace the symbol for infinity with your finger three times and each time, as you do so, say, "These two hearts are meant to be as one. These two hearts shall beat as one. These two hearts are forever one."

Meditate on your togetherness for a few minutes. Then, move the candles together onto the paper in the middle. Combine their flames so they are as one and say, "As I will it, so it is!"

Let the candles burn out.

Gather the refuse and place it in a bag or box with some hairs from both of you. Rub the hairs between your palms so it makes something like a fiber. You can, also, add nail clippings from both of you. Place it all in the bag or box. Then, put it some place where it won't be found by anyone, not even you, for a very long time. You can, also, bury it in your yard near your house.

Bringing your lover closer to you is the first step in dealing with interference. If the troublemakers are in your house, you must get them out.

If you have the fairly common problem of overbearing in-laws, friends or other house guests who overstay their welcome, you should follow up this spell with *To Get People Who are Interfering with Your Relationship Out of Your Home.*

You may, also, adapt some of the spells in *Chapter 13: Spells to Banish Unwanted Persons* and apply them to any unwanted guests to get them out of your house and out of your life.

To Get People Who are Interfering
with Your Relationship Out of Your Home

You will need the following:

Onion
Small piece of paper
Red taper candle
Glass of water (use a glass you don't mind breaking)

Burn the tip of the red candle, then break or cut it into three equal pieces and drop it into a glass of water. At midnight, stand in front of your house, facing it so you can look at it. Hold the glass with the water and candle pieces in it and say, "In the name of the Father, in the name of the Son, in the name of the Holy Ghost."

Shake the glass three times violently up and down and the third time smash the glass on the ground and break it. Then, say, "Dismiss this man (or woman) from this place." Enter your house through a different door and by a different path than the way you left it.

If the person you want to get rid of is a man, choose an onion that has a long shape to it. If the unwanted person is a woman, choose an onion that has a flat, squat shape to it. Cut a small hole in the top of the onion. Write the person's name five times on the paper and place inside. Then, replace the piece you cut out.

The next time the person leaves the house, make sure he or she is the very last to leave. Then, roll the onion across the threshold while wishing for him or her to leave. The unwanted person should depart in less than two weeks time.[5]

Meditation Spell to Welcome a Child to a Union

This is a powerful meditation to contact the spirit of your future child. You and your partner should be united for this purpose. On the night of a full moon, together with your partner, set aside about 15 minutes to speak to the spirit of your yet unborn child.

Tell the child that you are ready to welcome him or her into your life with unconditional love. Envision your child and address him or her directly, reach out through time and space and communicate anything you want to say. Speak from your heart. Do this for about 15 minutes upon the night of a full moon until you are able to conceive.

After you do this, massage each others hands and feet up to the ankles and legs using a massage oil. There are pressure points in the hands and feet which, when stimulated, help with erectile dysfunction. There are points on women's legs, particularly around the knees and the upper calves which help regulate a healthy hormonal balance.

CHAPTER 10
SPELLS TO REUNITE LOVERS

If you and your lover have parted for any reason or if he or she is just far away, these spells are designed to bring you back together.

Columbine Blossoms Lover Return Spell

Use this spell to bring back a wandering lover:

You will need the following:

7 Columbine blossoms, dried
7 Small bowls or glasses of water
Red image candle
Nail clippings, hair or bodily fluids from your beloved
Needle or thorn with which to make an inscription
Lover Return Oil
Patchouli incense
Flower Pot
Potting soil
Flower seeds
Your own bodily fluids

Anoint a red male or female image candle, which represents your lover. Inscribe the name of your lover upon it. Hollow out the bottom and insert the personal effects from this person along with some of your own bodily fluids. Anoint the candle and the personal items with Lover Return Oil. Then, seal the opening with melted wax.

Place each of the seven Columbine blossoms in a small bowl of water and arrange them in a circle around the candle.

Light the candle. Then, light the Patchouli incense. Speak to the candle as if you were addressing your lover. Say,"[Name], once you were by my side and soon you shall be, again." Tell the object what you want it to do exactly as if it were your lover.

Burn the candle for half an hour or so each day at the same time for, at least, nine consecutive days while visualizing your beloved returning to you.

When the candle has burned out, remove the personal effects from the bottom of the candle. Add some potting soil to the flower pot. Place the personal effects into the dirt along with a few drops of your own blood or saliva. Plant the seeds on top of this. Then, water the them and watch the plant as it grows. As it matures and blossoms, your lover will return and stay by your side.

An Old English Incantation
to Make a Lover Return

To make a lover return, throw a little salt into the fire on three successive Friday nights, while saying these words:

"It is not this salt I wish to burn,
It is my lover's heart to turn;
That he may neither rest nor happy be,
Until he comes and speaks to me."

On the third Friday night your lover should appear.[6]

To Summon the Intranquil Spirit and Make a Lover Return

The Intranquil Spirit is the spirit of a dead person damned to Hell and doomed to walk the earth, who is sent to torment a lover until he or she returns to you. This is a spell of last resort, used only the most dire cases in which your lover has left you and you fear he or she is never going to come back.

The Intranquil Spirit is actually one of many spirits who was wicked in life. They may be the spirits of rapists, murderers or robbers. Some of them are more helpful and easier to manage than others. If you find one who works well for you, ask for his or her name so the spirit can be summoned directly in the future.

The purpose of this spell is to send an unpleasant spirit to torment your wayward lover until he or she returns to you. Sometimes the person who casts this spell is, also, tormented along with the wandering lover. The limitation of this spell is that it does not necessarily make the person love you, it only sends a spirit to haunt them until they relent and return.

Summoning the Intranquil Spirit is a conjuration established by Mexican brujos and it is black magic. It is powerful and if you establish a relationship with a spirit that is helpful, he or she can help you with other problems that may arise. But, it is not a good spell for the novice or anyone who is weak-willed or easily frightened. It is, also, helpful to be well-versed in exorcism and defensive witchcraft.

Many practitioners warn against summoning the Intranquil Spirit inside your own home. Some of the spirits may become aggressive and your house could become haunted by the spirit of a violent criminal. For this reason, you may want to perform this summoning in a location outside your home. The grave site of a person known to have committed murder or some other heinous crime can be used. If you are concerned about being followed by evil spirits, make a point of crossing over running water before returning home.

You will need the following:

Black candle
Photograph, nail clippings, hairs, signature or bodily fluids
Needle or thorn with which to make an inscription
Glass of water
Intranquility Oil
White crucifix
Uncrossing Bath (Bay leaf, Hyssop and Sea Salt)

Anoint the photograph or other personal effects with Intranquility Oil. Inscribe the wayward lover's name onto the candle. Place the anointed item beneath it, in a hollow in the bottom of it or, if this is not feasible, in front of it on your altar.

Light the candle. Place the glass of water on the altar as an offering to the spirit. Spend a few minutes allowing yourself to relax and go into a meditative state. Then, hold the crucifix upright in your right hand as if you are brandishing it. With as much emotion as you can muster, recite the following incantation:

"O, Intranquil Spirit,
You that in Hell are wandering and will never reach Heaven,
Hear me! O, Hear me!
I command you to grasp the five senses of [Name].
Give him no peace, neither seated nor standing, waking nor sleeping;
Oppress and torment him with darkness and despair;
Allow him no peace, neither seated, standing or sleeping;
That he should find himself as restless as the waters of the seas;
That he should run until he humbly falls at my feet because nobody would help him;
Neither a divorcee nor a married woman nor a widow should love him;
I conjure you before this cross and God, that [Name] is to run after me as the living after the cross and the dead after the light. Amen."

Sit meditating for a few minutes. Allow the candle to burn out. Then, place the items used in this spell into a bag or box and bury them. If you are already in the cemetery, this is an ideal place. Once you've done this, forget the whole affair as if it had never happened and return home without looking back.

Once you have arrive home, prepare yourself a cleansing bath of Bay Leaf, Hyssop and Sea Salt. You may add a few drops of Lavender and Rosemary oil to enhance your relaxation and raise your vibratory rate.

Santa Muerte Spell to Make a Lover Return

Santa Muerte is commonly called upon to make a lover return. This spell is a novena to be repeated over a period of nine nights at a time when you believe your beloved is asleep and more vulnerable to its influences. This spell is similar to the previous one, but not as dark or dangerous.

To do this spell, you will need :

Red Santa Muerte candle
Lover Return Oil
Red ribbon
Photograph of your lover with his or her name written on the back of it
Santa Muerte prayer card (or image of her printed from the internet)
Red or black altar cloth
Cross

The cross in this spell can be any kind of cross, including one with arm of equal length like the Celtic cross. If you don't have anything like this, tape two pencils together so they form a cross. Fundamentally, the cross is a symbol of the four directions and the four elements.

Prepare your altar with a red cloth to represent the love as well as the domination and the torment you wish to impose upon your wayward lover. Alternatively, you may use black, letting it represent the absorption and destruction of any negative energies, which might impede this working.

Anoint the candle with Lover Return Oil. If it is a pull-out candle, you will be able to remove the candle from the glass holder and rub it with oil. Otherwise, poke a few holes in the wax on top and pour some Lover Return Oil into the openings.

Place your red Santa Muerte candle upon the altar along with the other items you will need for this spell. Light the candle.

On the first night of this spell, tie the photograph and the image of Santa Muerte to the cross with a red ribbon leaving a tails on the ribbons long enough for you to tie nine knots in them. Grasp both tails and tie a knot in them as if they were one. Tie only one knot per night over the course of the days of the novena. Each time, say a prayer to Santa Muerte and make your petition.

Invoke her presence as follows:

"O, Most Holy Death, please relieve me of all envy, poverty and hate. Enlighten my home with your holy presence. I ask that you break and destroy any curses that may have been placed upon me or my home. Bless me with love, prosperity and good health. Bless all those who live in my home with peace, health and well-being. Santa Muerte, you are my protector. Shield me from my enemies great and small. Destroy those who would harm me or my house. [Insert your petition.] Amen."

Your petition doesn't have to be an incantation. It can be any statement of your desires in the situation.

The following is only given as an example:

"Most Holy Death, forsake me not.
Cloak me in your mantle of protection
and do not give [Name] a moment of peace.
Let him be in misery and doubt.
Let him worry and bother himself
until he returns to me. Amen."

When the novena is complete, place the items from this spell in a box or bag and put it in a drawer or in the back of a closet where you won't think about them, again.

Hoodoo Spell to Bring Back a Lover No. 1

If your lover has left you and you want him or her back, use this spell.

You will need the following:

6 Red candles
7 Small squares of paper
384 Straight pins

Stick 60 pins into each candle, placing 30 on each side. As you stick in each pin say, "'Tumba Walla, Bumba Walla, bring [Name] back to me."

Write your lover' name three times on one of the papers.

Burn one of the candles prepared with pins each night for six consecutive nights, placing the paper with your lover's name under the candle as it burns. Each morning take up the sixty pins left from the burning of the candles and save them.

After you have burned each of the candles, write your lover's name once on one of the remaining six pieces of paper. Stick four pins in them arranged in such a way as to "box in" your lover by placing one pin on all four sides of the name. Then, collect the candle remains, paper and pins and put them in a bag or box and bury this in a hole near or beneath your threshold.

The piece of paper with the name written on it three times, upon which each candle stands while burning, must be kept each day until the last candle is burned. Then, bury it in the same hole with the rest of the remains. [7]

Hoodoo Spell to Bring Back a Lover No. 2

You will need the following:

Small piece of paper
Soiled sock, which he or she has worn on the left foot
Red candle
Sprig of fresh Sweet Basil
Glass of water
Metal barrel

This entire procedure must be done secretly. Write his or her name three times on the paper. Dig a hole in the ground. Place the paper with the name on it into the hole first. Then, place the sock in the hole. Place a red candle on top of this. Place a sprig of Sweet Basil into a glass of water and place it behind the candle.

Light the candle at noon and burn until 1 p.m. Light it again at 6 p.m and burn it until 7 p.m. Always snuff out the candle with a snuffer; do not blow it out.

Each time after the candle is lit, cover the hole with a metal barrel. Once it is place, knock on it three times to call the spirit and say: 'Tumba Walla, Bumba Walla, bring [Name] home to me."[8]

Angela Kaelin

CHAPTER 11
COMMANDING SPELLS

Use these spells to modify the behavior of your lover and bring him or her under your command.

To Dominate a Man or Woman

If you wish to dominate a lover and make him or her bend to your will, use this spell.

You will need the following:

Red, pink or white candle
Photograph of the person you wish to dominate
Needle or thorn with which to make an inscription
Bend Over Oil
Bend Over Powder or Domination Powder

Obtain a photograph of the person you wish to dominate in which he or she is alone in the photograph without the influence of others.

Inscribe the person's name on the candle nine times in a spiraling fashion. Anoint it with Bend Over Oil.

Sprinkle the photograph with Bend Over Powder or Domination Powder.

Relax and allow yourself to go into a mild trance. Then, addressing the photograph, speak to the person as if you were talking to them face to face. Your objective is to make telepathic contact. Address him or her by name and say:

"[Name], bend over because from this point forward, I control you and you will behave exactly like I want you to."

Then, place the photo in the bottom of your right shoe face up. Thereafter, the person will be compelled to do what you want them to.

Classic Bend Over Spell to Dominate Your Lover

Use this spell to dominate your lover.

You will need the following:

Red figure candle to represent your lover
Photograph, signature, hair or nail clippings
Small piece of paper
Needle or thorn with which to make an inscription
Bend Over Oil
Bend Over Powder

Write your lover's name nine times in a column on the paper, then turn it 90 degrees and cross and cover it by writing, "Bend Over," nine times over the top of the first column.

Inscribe his or her name onto the candle. Carve out the bottom of it and place the photograph, signature, hair, fingernail clippings or other small personal item belonging to him or her inside. Sprinkle a little Bend Over Oil or Bend Over Powder inside the space before sealing the opening with melted wax.

Anoint the candle with Bend Over Oil and rub it in, using a motion toward you, as you project your desires onto the candle. Envision what you want the person to do and how you want them to behave toward you.

Place the candle upon its holder. Dip the four corners of the paper into the Bend Over Oil. Sprinkle it with Bend Over Powder. Fold the paper toward you, keeping the powder in the middle, while imagining your desired outcome as you do so. Turn the paper 90 degrees and fold it one or two more times. Then, place it under the candle holder.

Sprinkle Bend Over Powder around the candle. Light it and let it burn all the way down. Bury the remains in your lover's backyard to exert your influence over him or her.

Spell to Create a Domination Sack

The Domination Sack, sometimes referred to as a 'Nation Sack, is a special kind of mojo bag traditionally used only by women and worn about the waist on a belt or cord. It contains the woman's power over her man, but he must never be allowed to touch it.

If your man has a wandering eye and you want to keep him from being able to perform with anyone else or if you want to increase his generosity toward you and generally keep him under your thumb, then you may benefit from creating a Domination Sack.

You will need the following:

Red candle
Needle or thorn with which to make an inscription
Piece of white paper
Red mojo bag
White cotton string no more than a 10" to 12" long
Incense of your choice
Personal effects and intimate bodily fluids
Photograph
Silver coins, other coins or 2 lodestones
Orris root (whole)
High John the Conqueror root (whole)
Follow Me Boy Oil, Domination Oil or Jezebel Oil

Optional ingredients:

Calamus root (whole)
Licorice root (whole)
Rosemary
Chili Pepper
Skullcap
Iron filings, if using lodestones
Optionally, other love charms, roots or talismans

The Domination Sack is a highly personal type of talisman, which may contain different items at your discretion. As you acquire the items need for this spell, decide if you would prefer to use lodestones or coins.

If you choose to use lodestones instead of coins, select two stones to represent yourself and your lover. Feminine lodestones are round in shape, while masculine lodestones have a longer, narrower shape. Baptize each stone and name it to represent each one of you by holding the stone while sprinkling water over it and saying, "I name you [Name] and I baptize you in the name of the Father, the

Son and the Holy Ghost." About once a week, feed the stones by sprinkling them with a pinch of steel filings or magnetic sand.

If you decide to use coins, there are different ways to select the coins for your Domination Sack. You may select a coin for each of you, which was minted the years you were born. If there is an age difference between you, you may use a number of silver coins that represents this number of years. Or, you may use nine silver dimes or a single silver dime that was minted in a leap year. Leap years occur every four years as follows: 1964; 1968; 1972; 1976, etc.

Without his knowledge, measure the man's erect penis with the string or with your fingers. Cut a piece of string to the exact same length. Collect a few of his pubic hairs and some of his semen. Then, once he has fallen asleep and you are out of his sight, slather the semen onto the string.

Tie nine very loose knots in the string beginning in the middle and working your way out, alternating right to left.

You must then tighten each knot in the order in which you made them. When you are ready to tighten a knot, call out the man's name. When he answers, cinch the knot tightly. This spell is done over the course of a few days and it can be strengthened by slathering more fresh semen onto the string before each tightening. It must be done in complete secrecy.

Place the lodestones or coins and the knotted string on your altar. On the piece of paper, write his name nine times in a column. Then, turn the paper 90 degrees and cover it with your own name written nine times in the same way to represent your domination of him.

Inscribe his name nine times in a spiral on the candle. Then, anoint it with your choice of either Follow Me Boy Oil, Domination Oil or Jezebel Oil while thinking of your desire. Place the paper underneath the candle. Addressing the candle, as if you were speaking to the person, say, "[Name], come to me, stay with me and come under my will."

Orris roots are used to represent a woman in this matter,

while High John the Conqueror roots are used to represent a man. If you are using a coin or lodestone to represent your lover, pair it with the appropriate root on the altar.

Anoint the coin or lodestone that represents your your lover and say, "This is [Name]." Do the same with the coin or lodestone that represents yourself.

Anoint the High John the Conqueror root the same way, then place it on or near the dime or lodestone. Do the same with the Orris root.

Place all of your lover's personal effects, the knotted string, the photograph and any optional charms, roots or talismans into the mojo bag.

Add nine drops of oil, one at a time. After each drop, say, "[Name], come under my will and do as I say."

Light the incense and pass the mojo bag through the smoke nine times in a motion toward you. Each time, say, "[Name], come under my will and do as I say."

Allow the candle to burn down. Then, take the paper and place it in the sack, again, saying, "[Name], come under my will and do as I say."

Collect the candle refuse and bury it in your backyard to keep its influence near your home.

When the Domination Sack is complete, do not tie the strings of the bag in a knot, but wrap them around and tuck the ends beneath the coiled strings and pull them tightly. This keeps the energy flowing freely and makes the bag easier to open. It must be fed about once a week by pouring a few drops of whiskey on it, passing it through incense or feeding it your own blood or fluids.

Keep it with you at all times. The best place to wear it is near your pubic region. If you are wearing a skirt, you can pin it inside and let it hang down. If you're wearing pants, place it in your pocket. It may, also, be worn on a cord around your neck, but it should be tucked inside your clothes so that no one will ever have the opportunity to see or touch it. If you sleep alone, you may wear it all night. But, when you sleep with your lover, you must lock it away where he will not be able to touch it. If he opens the bag or even touches it, the spell will be broken.

While the Domination Sack is traditionally used only by women, gay men have found success with it. In this case, it can be made exactly as described here. At your discretion you may use two High John the Conqueror roots instead of one High John and one Orris. In any case, it is important not to confound your own bodily fluids with those of the person you intend to dominate, lest you fall victim to your own spell.

This Domination Sack is based on the concept of the "Nation Sack" first recorded by Harry Middleton Hyatt in his travels through Memphis, Tennessee between 1935 and 1939.[9]

Dominate Your Man Spell

Use this spell to tie down your lover and keep him faithful.

You will need the following:

Blue male genitalia candle or taper
Red mojo bag
Needle or thorn with which to make an inscription
White cotton string no more than a 10" to 12" long
Personal effects and bodily fluids
Bend Over Oil or Domination Oil
Orris root powder

Just as in the procedure from the previous spell, use the string to secretly measure your lover's most intimate part while collecting bodily fluids and pubic hairs. Once you have the string cut to this length, tie nine knots in it, incorporating his hairs, fluids and personal effects. Save this string in a safe place where it will not be seen or touched by anyone else until a Tuesday night during the dark of the moon.

Then, inscribe your lover's initials onto the candle along with a command such as, "Only make love with me." Anoint it with Bend Over Oil. Notch the side of the candle, dividing it into seven equal sections. Place it in the candle holder. Sprinkle Orris root powder around it for added power.

Encircle the base of the anointed candle with the string. Burn the candle down to each notch over the course of seven nights until it is burned down completely. After you've completed this spell, place the string along with hairs and bodily fluids into a mojo bag. Keep it with you and never let anyone see or touch it.

To Get Revenge on an Unfaithful Man

If your lover disappoints you, use the knotted string you've created in the previous spells to get revenge by using it in this candle spell, which is intended to throw your lover into a state of pure misery and render him incapable of performing sexual acts with anyone.

Perform this spell on a Tuesday during a waxing moon, preferably in the hour of Mars.

You will need the following:

The knotted string
Black male genitalia, figure or taper candle
Double Crossing Oil (formula below)
Goofer Dust (formula below)

Inscribe your lover's name or initials onto the candle.

Then, slightly melt it and imbed the knotted, semen-soaked string into the wax, long ways from top to bottom, parallel with the wick.

Anoint the candle with Double Crossing Oil and sprinkle it with Goofer Dust. Light the wick and let it burn down completely, including the string. Bury the remains in a cemetery.

Double Crossing Oil

1 cup Almond oil
2 T. Valerian root
2 T. Stinging Nettles
2 T. Cayenne Pepper
1 T. Black Pepper
2 T. Patchouli

Combine the above ingredients into a jar with a lid. Place it in a warm spot and shake it twice per day for two weeks. Afterward, strain the liquid into a glass bottle.

Goofer Dust

1 part Graveyard dust, preferably taken from the grave of a murderer at midnight
1 part Cayenne Pepper
1 part Sulfur
1 part Ashes from a fire
1 part powdered Bones (bone meal)
1 part powdered Snake Skin
1 part Iron filings

Spell to Keep a Woman Faithful

Use this spell, if you would like to keep a woman faithful and true to you.

You will need the following:

Red female genitalia, figure or taper candle
Red mojo bag
Needle or thorn with which to make an inscription
Personal effects, pubic hairs and orgasmic fluid
Small, clean, white cotton cloth
High John the Conqueror root
Bend Over Oil
Bend Over Powder

Secretly gather a few of her pubic hairs along with orgasmic fluids on a white cotton cloth and place them into a red cotton bag. Add a whole, uncut High John the Conqueror root and a pinch of Bend Over Powder.

Inscribe her name nine times onto the candle. Anoint it with Bend Over oil. Place the bag with the items in it in front of the candle.

Light the candle. Allow yourself to go into a meditative state. With all the emotion you can muster, speak to the candle as if it were the person and say, "[Name], I command you that you shall always be faithful and true to me."

Allow the candle to burn down completely. Or, you may snuff out the candle and repeat this spell over the course of seven nights.

Afterward, remove the bag from your altar and keep it with you, preferably in your front pocket. Don't let anyone else touch it or else the spell will be broken.

Hoodoo Spell to Keep a Lover Home

If your lover is leaving home a lot for any reason and you want to keep him or her home, use this spell.

You will need the following:

Used, unlaundered sock
Small piece of paper
Silver dime or other small genuine silver coin
Some hairs from his or her head
Lodestone
Steel filings
Whiskey

Lay the sock belonging to your lover out on a table, bottom up.

Write your lover's name on the paper three times and put it on the sock.

"Place the dime on the name and the hair on the dime. Put a piece of 'he' Lodestone' on top of the hair and sprinkle it with steel dust. As you do this, say, 'Feed the he, feed the she.' That is what you call feeding the Lodestone. Then, fold the sock heel on the toe and roll it all up together, tight. Pin the bundle by crossing two needles. Then, wet it with whiskey and set it up over a door."[10]

To Stop Infidelity and Keep a Lover True

Anoint yourself with this oil before going to bed with your lover to keep him or her faithful. Make this potion on a Saturday.

1/2 cup Almond Oil
1 tsp. Allspice
1 tsp. Clove
1 tsp. Deer's Tongue
1 tsp. Mullein
1 tsp. Sage
1 tsp. Vetivert
1 tsp. Bed Sheet Ashes
7 drops Lime oil
7 drops Orange oil
7 drops Rose oil

Create Bed Sheet Ashes by burning a piece of one of your old, unlaundered bed sheets, which you have slept on together.

Combine the dried ingredients into a jar along with the Almond oil. Allow them to macerate for two weeks in a warm place out of direct sunlight. Afterward, strain the liquid, add the essential oils and bottle it. This oil can be used alone or added to hand and body lotions.

Caution: Applying citrus essential oils to the skin has been known to cause skin pigmentation changes in some people when the area is exposed to the sunlight.

Spell to Draw a Man's Passion to Yourself
and Cause Him to Forsake All Others

This spell comes from the practices of the strega of Italy, as documented by Charles Godfrey Leland in the 19th century.

You will need the following:

3 Indian chestnuts or wild horse-chestnuts (marroni d'Indi or marroni selvatici), powdered
New, unused pot
3 drops or more of blood or other bodily fluids from the man or woman involved
Pint of Water
Pint of Grain Alcohol

Grind the Chestnuts to a powder and place them into the new pot. Add, at least, three drops or more of the blood of the straying lover or his paramour. Add a pint of water. Boil this mixture for 15 minutes.

Remove it from the heat, allow it to cool a little. Strain it. Stir in the alcohol. Then, place the liquid under the bed where you sleep with your lover. The following must be done three times per night for seven nights in a row beginning at midnight.

Leave the bed and bathe the man's head and testicles. Then, make the sign of the cross over his body and recite the following incantation:

"I bathe not thee, I bathe thy heart,
That thy love from me may ne'er depart!
That thou shalt to me be true for aye!
Nor with other women go thy way,
Nor deal with them, be it as it may."

After the seventh night, throw the pot and all its contents into a running stream, saying:

"Now I cast this pot away,
With my husband's thought to stray,
To others' love that I may see
Him true, as I shall ever be!"

After you have thrown it into the water, walk away without looking behind you, and for three days after do not pass by that place."[11]

CHAPTER 12
BREAK UP SPELLS

The heart wants what it wants, it is said. If your true love is in the wrong relationship, these spells are intended to set things right.

To Break Up a Couple

Use this spell to break up a couple.

You will need the following:

2 Small pieces of paper
2 Lemons
Vinegar

Write each person's name eight times on a separate little piece of clean white paper.

Cut off the ends of the lemons. Poke a hole through the middle of each one, long ways, where you've made the cuts.

Roll up each of the papers into a little scroll. Insert one of them into each one of the lemons. Then, bury them together in a sunny spot in your yard where they will rot in the heat. Each day at the same hour, pour a cup of vinegar on the spot where they are buried.

Soon the two will begin fighting and separate from each other.

Black Candle Divorce Spell

Use this spell to cause divorce between a married couple.

You will need the following:

2 Black image candles, tapers or divorce candle
Picture of the couple or paper with their names on it
Needle or thorn with which to make an inscription
Separation Oil

Inscribe the name of each party onto their respective candle or the appropriate area of the candle, if you are using a divorce candle.

Anoint each candle with Separation Oil using a twisting motion. Then, light it.

If you have a picture of the couple, use this. Otherwise write each person's name on opposite ends of a piece of paper.

Anoint the edges of the photograph or paper.

Then, hold the photograph or paper in your hand and recite the following incantation:

"As these candles burn away to nothing, so burns away the bond between [Names], never to be formed again."

Allow the candle to burn down completely. Bury the refuse at a crossroad near the couple's dwelling place. After you do this, return home without looking back.

Hoodoo Spell to Break Up a Couple
and Send One Out of the House

Use this spell to break up a couple and send one of them away. You must have permission to enter the couple's home to perform this spell.

You will need the following:

Lemon
Salt
Piece of paper
Red Pepper

Write down the names of the couple nine times on a piece of paper. Cut a small hole in the stem end of the lemon and pour salt inside. Roll up the paper and place it inside.

Find a place in the yard of the couple's house where the sun shines very hotly. Dig a small hole and bury the lemon with the bloom side up.

Inside their home, throw some Red Pepper into the oven. Then, scatter salt in each corner of the house, especially the bedrooms and underneath the bed. As you do this say, "Just fuss and fight until you part and go away."[12]

Separation Spell

Use this spell to separate a couple. It is best begun on a Saturday night during a waning moon.

You will need the following:

2 Black figure candles
Separation Oil
Separation Powder

Inscribe the name of each party onto the candle that represents him or her. Anoint the candles with Separation Oil using a twisting motion.

Arrange the candles with about an inch between them, facing outward away from each other.

Sprinkle Separation Powder in a circle around the candles and say:

"Once thick as thieves; now bitter as bile. No more unity; only enmity between [Name the people involved]. You get on each others nerves; in each others hair. You hate each other and will separate and depart from each other. So it is!"

Let the candles burn for a little while before snuffing them out. Perform this ceremony for nine consecutive nights, moving the candles a little further away from each other each time you do it.

At the end of this spell, take the refuse and bury it at a crossroad near their home. If it is possible, sprinkle Separation Powder or Separation Oil where they must walk through it or come in contact with it. Be subtle.

Spell to Break Up a Couple
and Take One as a Lover

If you wish to break up a couple and take one of them for your own, conduct this spell twice per lunar cycle; once as the moon wanes and again when the moon waxes. Begin this spell as the moon wanes at a time of night when you believe the couple to be asleep.

You will need the following:

Black pillar or divorce candle
Red candle
Rusty nail with which to make an inscription
Separation Oil
Small jar with a lid
2 or 3 Chicken hearts
Graveyard dirt
Valerian root
Cascara Sagrada
Red mojo bag
Rose petals
Lavender, dried
Cinnamon powder
Piece of paper
Photograph, nail clippings or small personal item

If it is possible, obtain a photograph of the couple together and something personal belonging to each person in the couple, such as unlaundered underwear, nail clippings or hair. If you cannot obtain these things, write each person's name on the same piece of paper, then tear it in two so that one name remains on each half of the paper.

Inscribe the names of the couple onto the black candle. Using a twisting motion, anoint it with Separation Oil while envisioning the couple breaking up.

Then, light the candle. Speak to it as if you were addressing the minds of the couple. Imagine you are a hypnotist and they are under hypnosis, deeply relaxed and highly receptive to your suggestions.

Recite the following incantation:

"As this candle burns out, so burns out the flame of love. Now you are two broken hearts, soon to part and go your separate ways."

Into the small jar with the lid, combine the chicken hearts with the Graveyard Dirt, Valerian root and Cascara Sagrada. If you have personal items belonging to either of the couple, add them to the jar. Rip the photograph of the couple or the paper with the names on it in half, so that each person's image or name appears on separate pieces of it. Put the half that represents the person you want to get rid of into the jar with these items.

Keep the half of the photo or paper that represents the person you want to take as a lover. Also, retain some of his or her personal effects, if you have them. Put these in a safe place.

Recite the following words over the jar:

"Your appeal is gone. You wallow in decay. Soon you will wither entirely away."

When the candle has burned down, gather the refuse from this spell and place it in the jar. Bury it at a crossroad near the home of the person you want to leave this situation. As the contents of the jar fester and rot, the spell will begin to take effect.

On the night of a waxing moon, when you believe the one you love to be asleep, perform the last half of this spell.

Anoint the red candle with Come to Me Oil using a motion toward you. Place the photograph of your beloved in front of the candle along with any personal effects.

Light the candle and speak to it as you did before. Address the person by name as if he or she were in front of you and in a hypnotic sleep.

Recite the following words:

"[Name], come to me. Be with me. Love me."

When the candle has completely burned down. Place the photo and personal items into a red mojo bag. Add a few Rose petals, a pinch of Lavender and a pinch of Cinnamon. Sprinkle three drops of Come to Me Oil into the bag. Make a cross in the air three times over the bag.

Then, recite the following incantation over the little bag:

"You are my love and with me you shall be by the power of three times three."

Place the bag inside your clothing close to your heart and wear it every day. Place it under your pillow at night.

Gather the remains of the red candle and bury them in your own backyard or keep them in a drawer or closet.

Angela Kaelin

CHAPTER 13
SPELLS TO BANISH UNWANTED PERSONS

Unwanted persons take many forms and may include ex-lovers, persistent co-workers, street harassers, unwelcome house guests and overbearing in-laws. Use one of these spells to solve your problem.

Banishing by Fire Spell

To banish an unwanted lover or other pest, conduct this spell during the waning moon.

You will need the following:

Thurible or small iron cauldron
Garlic
Nettles
Rue
Photograph, personal effects or a piece of paper

Combine equal parts of Garlic, Nettles and Rue in a thurible. Add the photograph or personal effects belonging to the person, if you have them. If not, write the person's name on a small piece of paper.

As you burn these objects, muster all of your anger and frustration at the person and recite the following incantation:

"I do not want you.
Go away and stay away!
Leave me alone!
Never return!"

Hot Foot Powder

Hot Foot Powder is a classic formula for getting rid of unwanted people.

1 cup Graveyard dirt
1/4 cup Sea Salt
1/4 cup Black Pepper
1/4 cup Cayenne Pepper
1/4 cup Sulphur
1/4 cup High John the Conquer

Combine the above ingredients in a grinder or a coarse mortar and pestle. Mix and pulverize them.

Sprinkle this powder where the troublesome person will have to walk through it. It is often laid down on the porch or sidewalk of an enemy to make him or her leave a place.

Spell to Stop an Abusive Man

If you are a woman in an abusive relationship with a man, ask St. Rita for help. She protects women from abusive men. This spell is best performed on a Sunday, but it can be done any time.

You will need the following:

St. Rita statue, prayer card or medal
White candle
Needle or thorn with which to make an inscription
Personal effects, such as hair or nail clippings

If your husband is very controlling, you may have difficulty finding time to do this. If you can, lock the door when you take a bath. Take care not to arouse his suspicions.

Secretly obtain a few of his hairs or nail clippings. Make a hollow in the bottom of a white candle and place them inside. Seal the opening with a little melted wax.

Then, inscribe your petition onto the side of the candle. For example, "St. Rita, make him stop his aggression immediately or else leave this house forever."

Place your image of St. Rita by the candle. Then, light the candle and focus on what you want to happen. Let your emotions pour forth while you meditate on this. Speak to St. Rita like she is a close friend to you. Ask for guidance and a peaceful end to your troubles.

This spell can help keep things calmer until you have the opportunity to put a complete end to the situation you find yourself in.

It is not a good idea for a man to use this spell because St. Rita favors women over men. She will work for a man, but he must be nearly perfect. Whenever she is invoked in a marriage, divorce often follows.

After you have worked this spell, you may want to perform another banishing spell to get him out of your house.

Spell To Obtain Freedom from a Controlling Person

Perform this spell to free yourself from a dominating person.

You will need the following:

9 black candles
Black cloth poppet
Needle, thorn or rusty nail with which to make an inscription
Photograph of the person
Personal effects such as hair or nail clippings
2 Straight pins
Fireplace, a large cauldron or other safe device for burning items
The Devil card from an old tarot deck
Banishing Oil

To make the poppet, you will need the following

Piece of black cotton or flannel
Pair of scissors
Straight pins
Needle
Black thread
Mullein or Spanish Moss

Trace the figure of a gingerbread man about 7" tall on a piece of cloth. Draw a 1/2" margin around the edge of the original outline.

Place another piece of the cloth underneath and pin them together. Cut around the outer line of the drawing.

Begin stitching at the top of the head and work your way all the way around leaving an opening large enough to insert the herbs. Include whatever personal effects you have. Then, stitch the head of the poppet closed.

If you do not have an old tarot deck, you may use an image of a Devil tarot card printed from the internet.

Inscribe the unwanted person's name onto each of the nine candles. Then, anoint the candles, the corners of the Devil card image, the photograph and the poppet with Banishing Oil.

Attach the tarot card and the photograph to the poppet with the two straight pins. Arrange the candles in a circle around the poppet. Charge this entire arrangement. Light the candles. Then, summon all of your anger, as you recite the following incantation:

"You will leave me alone, [Name]!
Once and for all!
You! [Name], shrivel up and die!
You! [Name], disintegrate to ashes and be scattered on the winds.
So shall it be!"

Allow the candles to burn down completely. Place the poppet in a fireplace or other fire safe container and set it on fire. As you watch it burn visualize the person's control being destroyed. Afterward, gather the ashes and other refuse from this spell and toss it into a river or stream. Watch it disappearing, moving away from you for a few moments. Then, turn and walk away without ever looking back.

Quitting Powder to Stop Harassment

To stop harassment in a certain place, sprinkle this powder around the harasser's customary area. For example, if you are being harassed at work, scatter this powder around the perpetrator's office or work space. To stop general harassment, place this mixture in a little cloth bag and carry it with you.

Combine equal parts of the following ingredients and pulverize them:

Chili Powder
Cinnamon
Mint
Nutmeg
Powdered Newsprint
Tobacco Ashes

Four Thieves Vinegar Spell to Banish a Pest

Use this spell to make a bothersome person person go away.

You will need the following:

Four Thieves Vinegar (formula below)
Piece of paper
Picture of the person
Bottle with a cork or a tightly fitting lid

Write the name and birth date of the person on a clean piece of white paper. Place the picture on top of it and roll them up together into a scroll.

Insert this into the bottle. Pour Four Thieves Vinegar into it. Cork the bottle or screw the lid down tightly. Then, toss it into a swiftly moving stream or river as you visualize the person moving away from you.

Four Thieves Vinegar

Vinegar
Hyssop
Lavender
Melissa (Lemon Balm)
Peppermint
Sage
Thyme
Garlic cloves

Combine and crush equal parts of the above herbs in a mortar and pestle. Place the herbs in a quart jar with a lid. Pour enough vinegar into the jar to just cover the herbs, then pour in more so that the herbs sit in the lower 1/3 of the jar and the other 2/3 of the volume of the jar is comprised of vinegar.

Tighten the lid on the jar and store it in a warm place out of the direct rays of the sun. Shake it twice per day for two weeks. Then, strain the liquid through a piece of cheesecloth or gauze and bottle your Four Thieves Vinegar.

To Forget a Love Affair and Move On

This is a highly effective method for regaining control over a situation and banishing obsessive thoughts, either about a lost love or the trauma from a relationship that was terminated because of abuse.

Write down whatever it is you are trying to forget on a small piece of paper. In the case of an ex-lover, write his or her name on a small slip of paper along with other identifying information such as birth date and address. Then, tear it into small pieces and throw it into the toilet bowl. Urinate on it before flushing it to the sewer.

You may have to do this several times, but it will eventually work. This same method can be used to get rid of all kinds of painful thoughts. Write down whatever bothers you and follow this same procedure.

To Banish a Lover

If your love affair has ended and you want to get the person out of your house and out of your life, use the following spell. You may apply it to anyone else in your home you want to evict. Begin this spell on a Saturday or during the dark or waning moon.

You will need the following:

Unlaundered underwear or socks belonging to the person
Bottle with a tight fitting cork or lid
Piece of a brown paper bag with no print on it
Black Salt or Sea Salt
Red Pepper
Sulphur

Secretly obtain a piece of recently worn underwear, socks or other article with the person's bodily fluids on it. Cut a strip of it and place it in a bottle. On a piece of an old brown paper grocery bag, write the person's name nine times in a column. Turn the paper 90 degrees and write "Timbuktu" nine times over the top of the names. Put it inside the bottle along with the remaining ingredients. Seal the bottle tightly and bury it. After nine days have passed, dig it up and throw it into a river or stream. Return home without looking back.

Hoodoo Track Spell to Banish an Unwanted Lover

Use this old spell to rid yourself of a worn out relationship.

Foot track dirt
Dark colored bottle with a wide mouth
Dirt from a mud dauber nest
Cayenne Pepper
Unlaundered sock belonging to the person

Collect the dirt of the right foot print of the person you want to banish and place it in a dark colored bottle.

Cook the dirt of this foot track together with the dirt from the mud dauber nest and Cayenne Pepper until it is "parched" or very dry.

Put this into the dirty sock and tie it up, turning the bundle away from you as you do so.

Carry it to a river or other body of flowing water at exactly noon. When you are within 40 feet of the river, run fast to the edge of the water, whirl suddenly and hurl the sock over your left shoulder into the water. Never look back, but say, "Go and go quick in the name of the Lord."[13]

Angela Kaelin

REFERENCES

1. Begy, Joseph A., "Practical Handbook of Toilet Preparations and Their Uses, Also Recipes for the Household,' New York: Wm. L. Allison, Publishing, 1889. Pp. 166-167.

2. Hurston, Zora Neale, "Mules and Men," 1935.

3. Leland, Charles G., "Etruscan Roman Remains in Popular Tradition," 1892. P. 145-146.

4. Leland, Charles G., "The Gospel of Aradia," 1899. P. 63.

5. Hurston, Zora Neale, "Mules and Men," 1935.

6. Lawrence, Robert Means, "The Magic of the Horse-Shoe With Other Folk-Lore Notes," 1898. http://www.sacred-texts.com/etc/mhs/

7. Hurston, Zora Neale, "Mules and Men," 1935.

8. Ibid.

9. Hyatt, Harry Middleton, "Hoodoo-Conjuration-Witchcraft-Rootwork; Beliefs accepted by many Negroes and white persons, these being orally recorded among Blacks and whites (Memoirs of the Alma Egan Hyatt Foundation) Vol. 2," Western Publ., 1970. P. 1458.

10. Hurston, Zora Neale, "Mules and Men," 1935.

11. Leland, Charles G., "Etruscan Roman Remains in Popular Tradition," 1892. P. 328-329.

12. Hurston, Zora Neale, "Mules and Men," 1935.

13. Ibid.

OTHER WINTER TEMPEST BOOKS

If you enjoyed this book, you might enjoy other Winter Tempest Books:

All Natural Dental Remedies: Herbs and Home Remedies to Heal Your Teeth & Naturally Restore Tooth Enamel by Angela Kaelin

Black Magic for Dark Times: Spells of Revenge and Protection by Angela Kaelin

Blood and Black Roses: A Dark Bouquet of Vampires, Romance and Horror by Sophia diGregorio (Fiction)

The Forgotten: The Vampire Prince by Sophia diGregorio

How to Communicate with Spirits: Séances, Ouija Boards and Summoning by Angela Kaelin

How to Develop Advanced Psychic Abilities: Obtain Information about the Past, Present and Future Through Clairvoyance by Sophia diGregorio

How to Read the Tarot for Fun, Profit and Psychic Development for Beginners and Advanced Readers by Angela Kaelin

How to Write Your Own Spells for Any Purpose and Make Them Work by Sophia diGregorio

Magical Healing: How to Use Your Mind to Heal Yourself and Others by Angela Kaelin

Natural Remedies for Reversing Gray Hair: Nutrition and Herbs for Anti-aging and Optimum Health by Thomas W. Xander

Practical Black Magic: How to Hex and Curse Your Enemies by Sophia diGregorio

Spells for Money and Wealth by Angela Kaelin

To Conjure the Perfect Man by Sophia diGregorio (Fiction)

Traditional Witches' Formulary and Potion-making Guide: Recipes for Magical Oils, Powders and Other Potions by Sophia diGregorio

Disclaimer: The author and publisher of this guide has used her best efforts in preparing this document. The author makes no representation or warranties with respect to the accuracy, applicability, fitness or completeness of the contents of this document. The author disclaims any warranties expressed or implied. The author of this book is not a medical or legal professional and is not qualified to give medical or legal advice. Nothing in this document should be construed as medical or legal advice. The material in this book is presented for informational purposes only. Nothing in this book should be construed as incitement to dangerous or illegal acts and the reader is advised to be aware of and heed all pertinent laws in his or her city, state, country or other jurisdiction. Any medical or legal questions should be addressed to the proper medical or legal authorities. The author shall in no event be held liable for any losses or damages, including but not limited to special, incidental, consequential or other damages incurred by the use of this information. The statements in this book have not been evaluated by any government organization. The statements contained herein represent the legally protected opinions of the author and are presented for informational purposes only. Anyone who uses any of the information in the book does so at their own risk with the understanding that the author cannot be held responsible for the consequences. This document contains material protected under copyright laws. Any unauthorized reprint, transmission or resale of this material without the express permission of the author is strictly prohibited.

FTC Disclaimer: The author has no connection to nor was paid by any brand or product described in this document with the exception of any other books mentioned which were written by the author or published by Winter Tempest Books.

www.ingramcontent.com/pod-product-compliance
Lightning Source LLC
Chambersburg PA
CBHW030933090426
42737CB00007B/414